passion for *coffee*

Patricia McCausland-Gallo

Cover design and composition: Rikki Campbell Ogden/pixiedesign, llc
Editorial services: Michelle Volpe-Kohler
Proofreading services: Joseph Sheffer
Photography assistance: Erik Simmons and Isabella Gallo

Production and Manufacturing: Favorite Recipes© Press

An imprint of
FRP
P.O. Box 305142
Nashville, Tennessee 37230
1-800-358-0560
www.frpbooks.com

Library of Congress Control Number 2007933958

ISBN-10: 0-9797594-0-4
ISBN-13: 978-0-9797594-0-6

Manufactured in China

Library of Congress Cataloging-in-Publication Data is available.

to Jorge Gallo & Violy Dieppa

I dedicate this book to two of the most important people in my life, my husband and my mother. To my mother for teaching me all I know about baking, and to my husband for teaching me about a life full of inner peace.

thank you

To Andrés Echeverri, the Colombian National Coffee Federation, The Caldas Coffee Committee, Ciro Bonilla V. and Marcelo Jaramillo T. of the Freeze Dried Coffee Company in Chinchiná, Caldas. To the coffee growers Cesar Mejía, Alfredo Restrepo, and Gilberto Pérez. To the Coffee Coop of Manizales, Juan Carlos Alarcón, Sandra Quiñones, and Hector Eli. To the Coffee Institute of Costa Rica, ICAFE and Fransisco Serracín of Pachi Estates in Panamá, and the Specialty Coffee Association of Panamá.

table of contents

introduction

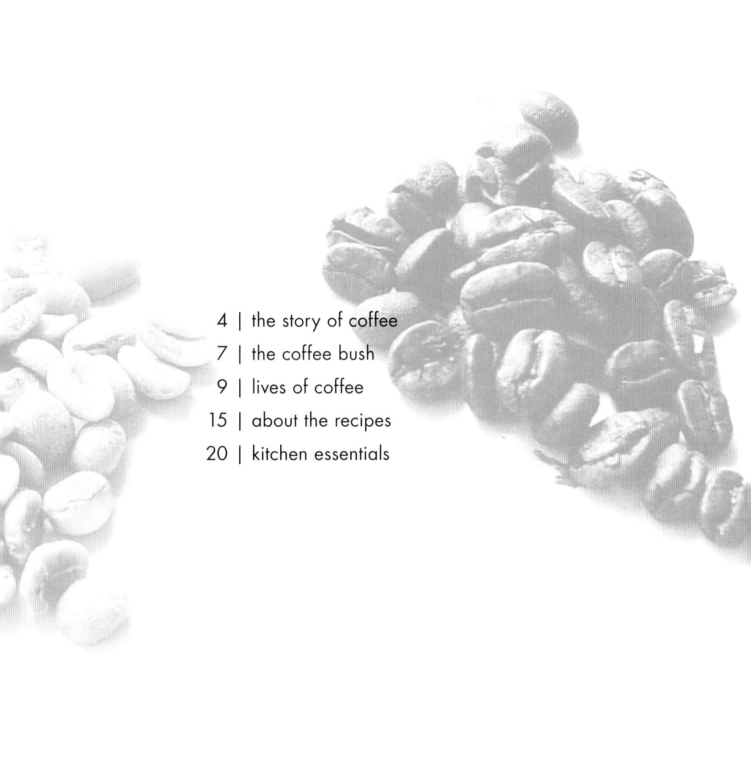

the *story* of coffee

The story of coffee begins with a colorful legend from Africa—in ancient Ethiopia, in the area of the modern Kaffa province, where the coffee tree probably originated. A goat herder named Kaldi, the myth begins, noticed that after his tired goats ate red berries from a tree similar to the bay laurel tree, they were lively and energetic until late in the evening. He then tried the magical red berries himself, which we know today as Arabica coffee, and experienced the same effect. Kaldi mentioned these events to the monks of a nearby monastery, who, from then on, ate the berries to stay awake during their nightly prayer gatherings. By chance, the legend continues, the monks discovered that the beans could be roasted, and that a beverage prepared from the roasted beans not only produced the same stimulating effect, but also tasted much better. Consumption of this beverage spread among the monasteries of the area and to neighboring mosques and Muslim regions where alcohol was forbidden. Even though not everyone embraced this new drink, coffee was now generally regarded as a luxurious stimulant.

The legend and the beans spread from Ethiopia to the great port of Moka on the Red Sea and the Gulf of Aden into Yemen and the Arabian peninsula, where it was cultivated and from where the Arabica coffee variety takes its name. Middle Eastern legends talk about a black beverage that inspires love and loyalty, heals the sick, comforts the exhausted, and allows long nights of prayer and meditation. By the sixteenth century, it was transported to Turkey and the rest of the Ottoman Empire. There, it was roasted on bonfires, acquiring its color and a wonderful aroma that spread through the air of Muslim lands, carrying the secrets, they believed, to achieving health, strength, and virility. Coffee drinking became widespread. The bean then continued its journey toward Persia, Egypt, Syria, and Europe.

Venetian traders first brought coffee across the Middle East and north into Europe during the sixteenth century. Initially, mystery enveloped this almost-sacred substance, with its reputation for endowing virility and strength. Possibly because of its rarity (cultivation was not feasible in northern climates), the European elite considered roasted beans a gift fit for royalty. This made coffee very attractive to those in the high political and religious spheres of society. Despite objections from the Catholic Church (but later with Pope Clement VIII's blessing), coffee consumption rapidly expanded throughout Europe. Its high price initially made it a drink of the wealthy and powerful—nobles, artists, intellectuals, and scholars—and by the end of the seventeenth century many coffeehouses

had sprung up all over the continent. Coffee had become synonymous with good service and warm welcomes.

Coffee then found its way to Southeast Asia, as well as the Americas. The Dutch are credited with cultivating and bringing the plant to their plantations in Ceylon and Indonesia. The Dutch are also credited with bringing the bean to Brazil, Venezuela, and Colombia—the cuisine of which has inspired the recipes in this book—via their possessions in the East Indies. It is believed that the French and British also planted coffee trees in their colonies. Some accounts tell of a French infantry captain who traveled on a ship to the "new world" carrying 15 coffee trees, of which only one survived. This single bush could be the origin of all of the coffee cultivated today in Central and South America. It seems that the plant then spread, over the course of thirty years, from Martinique to the Dominican Republic to Puerto Rico, and then finally arrived in Costa Rica and Panama.

March 16, 1780 is the earliest recorded date of coffee entering Panama, with 25 pounds of what historians think were seeds imported from Cartagena, Colombia. The first record of a coffee plant in Panama dates back to 1790, on the farm of Don Pedro de Ayarza in the Caribbean port of Portobello. The first coffee shop in Panama opened in 1822 and, shortly after that in 1836, the first eight *quintales* (46 kilograms) from the province of Chiriquí were exported. Within fifty years, coffee growing took off in the area of Chiriquí, where by 1882, 2,000 *quintales* of coffee were harvested in an area of 380 hectares. Coffee growing in Panama was never easy because of the small size of the territory, and this resulted in cultivation

5

changes and, consequently, a focus on specialty coffees, luxury coffees, and organic coffees.

According to Jose Chalarca (*Vida y hechos del café en Colombia*, Federación Nacional de Cafeteros de Colombia, 1998):

> *"Some believe that the first seeds or plants arrived in the states of Norte de Santander and Santander [Colombia] from Venezuela to the east; others believe that coffee arrived from Central America through the Urabá region. The most authorized version about the planting of the first coffee seeds in Colombia is that of the Spanish Jesuit priest Jose Gumilla, who mentions in his work* El Orinoco Ilustrado *that coffee was planted at the Santa Teresa de Tabage mission, which was founded by the Jesuits at the mouth of the Meta River, in the state of Orinoco, around 1730."*

In 1736, according to authorized sources, the Jesuits then carried the coffee seeds to Popayán and planted them in the seminary they owned in that city. Writes Chalarca:

> *"There were many accounts of coffee planting in the different regions of the country during the eighteenth century. The Viceroy Caballero y Góngora, in a letter dated 1787, stated that coffee grew well in all the regions of Girón (Santander) and Muzo (Boyacá); however, industrial cultivation of the plant only began during the third decade of the nineteenth century, as the first record of exportation, dated 1835, mentions 2,592 sacks weighing 60 kilos. It is also certain that such commercial cultivation first took place in eastern Colombia, in the region occupied today by the Santander states."*

Stories of love and romance carry coffee from French Guyana to Brazil. A Portuguese colonel, Francisco de Melo Palheta, arrived to resolve a frontier dispute between these two countries, and, at the time of his departure, his lover bade him goodbye with a bouquet in which she hid some fertile coffee seeds. Thus, as the story goes, the Brazilian coffee industry was born. The crop adapted so well to the local conditions that by 1938, Brazil had such a surplus of coffee that the government asked Nestlé to help preserve it; this request led the Swiss company to create its freeze-dried process, and Nescafe was born. (Though before this, the American scientist Satori Kato created the first instant soluble coffee in Chicago in 1901.)

Based on the earliest accounts of coffee, it has long been sought after for providing vitality, clarity, and virility. And later in its history, people began associating it with creativity and intellectualism. But it hasn't always been easy for coffee, of course: in Constantinople, there were people who did not embrace it, and, at times, Islamic and Catholic laws forbade it. Throughout its history, attempts were made to hide this small bean—a gift that sprouts naturally from the soil, whether arid or fertile—in order to control human beings. But perseverance over power allowed this natural and comforting beverage to be preserved. Coffee that helps us begin each morning's tasks, or stay awake throughout the night, with energy and clarity—just like it did for those goats in ancient Africa that first stumbled upon these magical beans.

the coffee bush

Coffee is a plant from the Rubiaceae family and bears the genus name Coffea. It is a small bush with dark, shiny leaves, small white flowers, and fruit that is green before it's ripe and a deep red when it's ready for picking. With more than 25 species—including new varieties introduced by man for cultivation under different environmental conditions—coffee lends itself to culinary creativity. In this book, I have used the wonderful properties of this bean to create a varied and exciting menu of sweet and savory foods.

The rewards of a well-kept coffee crop begin with carefully selecting the mother beans. After the beans are cultivated in a nursery, the seedlings are ready to be transferred to the land and nurtured. When the fruit, or cherries, become a rich, red color, they are carefully handpicked, and the long days and nights of tending to the plant only partially conclude.

Immediately after harvest, the thin, sweet layer that covers the berries must be removed. The white, sticky pulp underneath this layer, which covers the two coffee beans inside each berry, also must be removed. (In Colombia, the building where coffee beans are processed is called a *beneficiadero* or *beneficio*, "the benefit.") The waste generated from processing the beans is used as a fertilizer. The *bagasse*, the dry, fibrous residue of the beans, is sometimes passed through worm culture tanks that feed on it and, in return, produce fertilized soil.

Next, the beans are soaked in cold water for 24 hours, meticulously washed, and then dried, either in the sun or in drying machines that replicate the sun's heat. The beans are then inspected for overall quality, their history (*trazabilidad*) is recorded, and then they are taken to a laboratory where they are subjected to even more tests for quality. If the beans have been correctly produced, the farmer is authorized to bring the crop to the coffee plant, which is done via Jeeps, mules, or donkeys.

Once the crop reaches the coffee plant, the beans are inspected again by highly trained personnel. They remove the husks (the thin but tough parchment that covers the beans) of a few randomly selected beans and test them for aroma, size, texture, and other qualities. If the crop is approved for export, it is brought to a mill where all of the husks, or *pergamino*, are removed and then used as a source of energy for the machines.

Finally, the "cup tests," or "cupping," are performed, where a sample of the beans are roasted, ground, brewed, and tasted. If the coffee's aroma, flavor and other qualities don't meet certain standards, it will not be approved for exportation. "It's in the cups where one sees how much care the coffee grower has taken," says Juan Carlos Alarcón from the Chinchiná, Caldas (Colombia) Coffee Growers' Cooperative. "[This is] where one sees if he has been wise, if coffee is his life's priority . . . Through the cup one can describe [the coffee's] ancestry. By 'cupping,' one can identify if a bean has an imperfection: if this flaw has come from the picking process, the pulp-removal process, the tank, the drying process . . . and so on," adds Juan. Sandra Quiñones, an international cup jurist, offers, "Good coffee, excellent coffee, does not lose its quality whether it's served hot or cold; from the moment it is ground, one can sense its fragrance and aroma. Then in its flavor it is reaffirmed." These tests also establish the price that will be offered to the farmer.

The final product, *café pergamino*, as it is called in Colombia, or *café oro*, as it is called in Panama, is then shipped to distant lands where perhaps no one has ever seen a coffee plantation; to countries far away from and unknown to the people who cultivated the coffee so that we all may enjoy the best the land can offer.

lives of coffee

The coffee plant is the main character of the stories that follow—true stories in which people, enamored of the land and this crop, work tirelessly to produce the shiny, red berries that the plant yields only a few times a year. These are tales of the incredible path that many people choose to take in their lives, but that few others really understand.

All of the characters in these coffee stories share a common element, and it has inspired the name of my book: *Passion*. Everyone—from those who plant the seeds on just the right day; those who carefully pick only the beans that are ready for harvest; those who thresh each bean to remove the skin after a slow and exacting drying process; those who prepare meals and refreshments for the farmhands; to the executives of coffee companies—has a passion for their work, the land, and, most of all, coffee.

a humble beginning for a great journey

Antonio is a grown man, many years past the age of his retirement, but his love for coffee and the land on which it grows drives him to continue working. "I am from Aguadas, Caldas, and was brought [to this plantation] by an uncle when I was 18 years old," he told me. "I was illiterate and learned to sign my name when I was 22, with a teacher who taught me at night." Today, Antonio is the manager of a beautiful coffee farm.

When he first arrived at the plantation, Antonio learned to handpick coffee and tend to the mules that transport the fruit. His uncle moved from the area shortly after he brought Antonio there, and left the boy behind with the new farm owners. While he and the owners got to know each other, Antonio continued picking coffee and tending

9

to the mules. But the new owners had problems with the farm, and sold it. However, they recommended Antonio to the next owners, and he continued working hard and learning as much as he could about growing coffee.

After a while, Antonio married and had three children who grew up with him in the coffee fields. As his children grew, Antonio continued progressing in his job, eventually becoming the boss and driving a jeep. He taught his children how to drive and perform all of the tasks he knew how to do. "I would take them out to drive the jeep when they were 8 or 9; I loaded the car with wood and went out…and I would run into my boss who would ask if they had a driver's license…when I least expected it he would show up and would reprimand me, but thank God nothing eventful happened while we drove around these slopes."

Antonio loves this land. He studies it carefully, and schedules the plantings and *socas*, or cuttings, according to the phases of the moon. And he has learned from nature while cultivating the coffee, which has led him to employ agricultural biodiversity. He says that is why there are no large ant hills or pests in his coffee bushes. In addition to coffee, he grows trees and other crops, such as plantains, oranges, tangerines, lemons, Peruvian guava trees, passion fruit, corn, potatoes, and yucca. He farms because he

enjoys it, and because he knows that the fruits of the crops provide his family and the workers with their daily sustenance and the ingredients for refreshing beverages after a hard day's work. The workers who tend to the coffee live among the crops in white houses with red doors, a bounty of flowers, and impeccable kitchens. Coffee pickers work Monday through Friday, and on weekends they go into town to visit their families, have fun, and rest.

When we arrive at the *matarratón* trees on a hill above a schoolhouse, Antonio continues his story. "When the time came to send the first [son] to the army, my wife cried," he says. "I was happy. I told myself, 'Let them take him away and send him back a man, and teach him to be brave.'" He speaks happily about his children until he mentions his third-born child, and lowers his voice to talk about the motorcycle accident that killed his son a few months ago. I am accompanied by my daughter, Isabella, who is helping me take pictures, and I feel pain in the bottom of my heart.

All of sudden, a cell phone rings. For the first time that I've ever witnessed, this small device that has meddled so much with our lives rings at the perfect time, snapping Antonio back to life and happiness. It's his son-in-law asking if Antonio can come by and pick up him and his son. One can tell that Antonio likes to help others, and with a big

smile he replies that he will pick them up shortly. After his three-year-old grandson and son-in-law join us, we continue talking and taking pictures of the coffee bushes.

Once night falls, Antonio muses that, at his sixty-some years, he is healthy because "here [on the coffee lands], I get up at 5:30 and walk. The days go by without me noticing—I don't even feel the weeks. Sometimes, I don't even feel like going home. This land means everything to me."

family rules

Near the coffee fields is a small, white house where three sisters-in-law and their families live. It's a Friday afternoon and, since work and the day's chores are done, they are relaxing with their husbands and kids. The young children run around, while the older ones play hide and seek. The women laugh and play the noisy game, *tejo*, while others get ready to play soccer. They show us the soccer field, which is about 100 meters away on a mountain slope that's covered with coffee bushes and near a river.

During the week, Alicia, one of the sisters-in-law, and her husband, Pedro, rise at 6 a.m. After having breakfast with their children, a shower, and a cup of black coffee, they climb the nearby slopes to pick coffee. Alicia is drawn to the fields—they invigorate her. She has been picking coffee for about six years now. "During slow times, I pick fifty to sixty kilos," she says. She works mainly with men; there aren't many female coffee pickers, but they are respected and treated as equals: they work as much as the men.

At the end of each workday, Alicia returns home to her little Daniela who waits for her with open arms. In the evenings, she relaxes with Pedro and Daniela. They watch movies or soap operas, or just sit and enjoy the scenery. "I sing, dance, anything that comes up, we go to the soccer games—we do not have a team but we form one out on the patio. We make things up to remain active," she says, smiling. Paula and Cristina, her sisters-in-law, do not pick coffee. They stay at home and maintain the household, watch the children, and prepare delicious, peasant meals every day for the whole family. On Mondays, they usually prepare rice and eggs for breakfast and *sancocho* (a dish often made with chicken or fish, potatoes, corn, and cilantro) for lunch.

Close to their house is a chicken coop filled with beautiful, fat hens that will probably be part of a dinner in the near future. The children run around, in between their mothers' legs, not understanding why a couple of strangers with cameras and tape recorders are in their home. I can sense the settling of dusk and the official arrival of the weekend. The game of *tejo* continues, and I ask one of them to explain it: "I stand here and pick up a *tejo* [a four-inch, round metal disk that weighs a pound and a half], and I throw it to see if it 'burns wick'—that is, if it reaches a target marked with gunpowder and detonates it. The winner is the player who detonates or burns the largest number of wicks." My daughter and I stand and watch the game, and end up as absorbed in and excited about it as they are.

Pedro leaves the game and approaches us. He talks about how he arrived in the nearby city of Pereira eight years ago from an area halfway across the country. "Nobody can make me leave now," he says of these coffee lands. "What I like most is that I have a stable job; I don't have to go from farm to farm. And we have fun playing *tejo*, listening to music, singing, and living in the country."

the hands that feed

Argelia is a cook. She has a peaceful life; she spends her days in her garden and kitchen, and enjoys preparing delicious stews and breads for the coffee workers who come here every day to eat. She works Monday through Friday, and on weekends she prepares for the following week when she is told how many people will be working the fields. She is tall, dark-haired, and good-looking. Her white house has a tiled roof, red windows, and a red door. Flowerpots surround the house, and nearby she has planted plantains and peppers, as well as lemon trees for lemonade and wood for her kitchen. And hanging on her house is a cross made of bamboo, or what they call *guadua*, that is over two meters long.

In her spotless kitchen, Agrelia's pots, shiny as mirrors, hang on the wall waiting to be used. On the fire there are cast iron pots filled with steaming *sancocho*, rice, and thick red beans that she prepares daily, as they are a must for the evening menu. While we talk, she looks out the kitchen window at her daughter. Then she offers us some juice from guavas freshly picked from a tree in her garden, sweet and refreshing—perfect for an afternoon like today. When we walk to her field looking for ideal picture locations, we pass by her husband, silently sitting at a table—he is keeping her company today while he recovers from being sick. Her daughter helps with the afternoon chores and is never far from Agrelia, to whom we listen and photograph.

Argelia cooks daily on a fixed schedule for about 70 workers with big appetites. At dawn, she offers them a *tinto*, a hot cup of aromatic black coffee, to send them off to work. A couple of hours later, while it's still cold outside, it's breakfast time. She boils some water to make *agua de panela*, a cold, sweet beverage, and prepares thick, smooth chocolate for a hot beverage. She also bakes golden *arepas*, made of freshly ground corn, which she serves hot. This concludes the morning stage, which gives the workers strength to pick coffee until midday. When the sun is high and the air has warmed up, everyone returns to

Argelia's for lunch. The menu changes daily. Today it's the *sancocho* I saw cooking in her kitchen earlier today, with yucca, plantains, rice soup, pasta and meat; other days it's another comforting and nutritious favorite. Every day she sends the coffee pickers back to work loaded with energy after sharing a delicious meal cooked with care. When the sun sets and the workday is over, the workers return for supper. They remain at Argelia's until late, resting or playing *tejo* or cards, or simply chatting before returning home or to the bunks to sleep and then rise again at 5:30 a.m. to enjoy their send-off *tintos*.

the *alimentador*

Diego is the "provider," or *alimentador*, at the coffee farm. Although his title in Spanish implies that he is a "food provider" or "nourisher," Diego is not the person who prepares or delivers meals. His job is to look after the well-being of the farmhands while they're in the field and at the campsites. Diego is responsible, though, for making sure his workers receive their two daily *tintos*—the one that opens their eyes and hearts in the early morning, and the one that helps them relax after a long day of meticulous yet fulfilling work. He also offers them fruit juice or lemonade as refreshments.

Diego is slender, with fine features and chestnut-colored hair. He loves *tejo*, and cannot understand what my daughter and I are doing in such faraway and elevated lands, asking about people's work. I tell him that we want to get to know the people who live and work in the countryside, as we live and work in the noise of the city, far from nature. "Oh!" he says. "Well, if this helps to get

more people to come and work with coffee and to get to know us, then that is good." This sparks a conversation in which we begin learning about each other.

Diego's other responsibilities include accompanying the workers in the fields while they are picking so that they lack nothing, whether it's a tool or something to drink. He monitors how many people are working and what will be picked so that he may help distribute the workload. When the time comes at the end of the day to fill the sacks with ripe fruit, he hands out the bags and numbers they need to mark, store, and separate their bundles of coffee. Diego also bring groceries to the cooks and ensures that they have enough supplies to prepare hearty meals for his staff. Other tasks of his job include caring for the bushes and weeding. In short, Diego does a little bit of everything. His workweek ends on Friday, and on Saturday—payday—he

13

goes down to the city with his workers to calculate their wages, and then enjoys his weekend.

the town square and the *culebrero*

On holidays and weekends, there isn't a town square in the countryside that isn't visited by a *culebrero*—a sort of traveling magician, entertainer, and salesman. On this Saturday, not far from the coffee fields we toured during the previous week, it's not even noon and the square is crowded with people. There is no place to park—trucks, motorcycles, and cars fill all of the spaces across the square, and they even park in front of the nearby church.

It's a cool and sunny morning, a perfect setting for the magical realism that we're experiencing. Families holding small children by the hand cross the street, almost filling it completely from one side to the other. Affectionate youngsters stroll about with their dates. Grandfathers reminisce about when they, too, ran around the square on weekends and winked at the *señoritas* who strolled down the opposite sidewalk with their mothers. The grandmothers, on the other hand, sit with their grandchildren—the boys well groomed and the girls with braided hair and bows—introducing the children to their community where, one day soon, they will create their own lives. You see all kinds of people: some stroll peacefully and others are surprised; the youngest are bored, and the elderly are grateful for everything that life has given them, including these moments right here on the square.

Above the noise of the large crowd, we hear a voice that is noticeably louder than everyone else's. We get closer and, for the first time, meet the *culebrero* face to face.

At his feet is a box full of colorful stones. He wears a two-strand necklace of indigenous stones with an animal fang hanging in the center. His wavy, chestnut hair is covered by a modern blue-and-white bandana, and the rest of his outfit is like anyone else's—a sleeveless shirt and faded jeans.

He places a piece of dark cloth on the ground and displays accessories and charms of all sorts, as well as his valuable "healing stones." "I am not a wizard, I am not a magician, I am not a liar," he says. "I travel from town to town selling magical stones for your body's health, for love, and for life," he continues. With his charismatic voice, the *culebrero* seduces the people; they stop what they're doing and slowly crowd around him and listen in amazement.

A man picks up one of the small stones and carefully studies it; he wants to believe that it's actually different than a regular stone—a thought that perhaps everyone in the square, in the bottom of their hearts, would like to believe. The *culebrero* eventually departs, but he leaves everyone behind with a certain fantasy and hope that it is possible to find love, health, and peace from something in nature as ordinary as a stone.

getting to know coffee

High in the Andes Mountains of Colombia, on hills and near creeks, the richest coffee in the world is harvested. While incorporating Colombian coffee into some of my country's favorite foods, I have written this book for you, the coffee lover. *Passion for Coffee* is a comprehensive group of coffee recipes, as well as stories about coffee, the people who bring it to us, and the land on which it grows.

As I finished writing my previous book, *Secrets of Colombian Cooking*, thoughts of coffee began to waltz around in my mind. "Why," I asked myself, "if we have the best coffee in the world, are there no recipes in our cuisine that incorporate coffee?" A few months later, I began my journey with coffee at the baking station of my kitchen. The story of creating these recipes takes many twists and turns, with days of trial and error with many types of coffee—powdered instant, freeze-dried instant, freshly ground, freshly brewed, espresso, and more. I finally learned the best way to use each form of coffee to produce the most delicious, creamy, and aromatic coffee-infused recipes.

At first, I only thought of coffee in terms of sweets. Because of my background—I was born and raised in a home with a bakery that took up one-third of the house, with the ever-present scent of baking cakes mingling with the roasted coffee beans brewing in the back—I was ready to take on the world with delicious, sweet recipes made with the beloved coffee we all enjoyed. At my mother's bakery, which had a very French and avant garde ambiance, we blended thick, heavy creams, long vanilla beans, and different kinds of smooth, dark coffee beans to prepare extraordinary coffee mousses and coffee ice creams. These experiences influenced the sweet recipes I created for this book.

15

introduction

Later on in the recipe-development process, I ran into a friend who tempted me to write savory recipes with coffee, too. Of course, I said yes at once, but that was just an automatic response. As I wondered how in the world I was going to fulfill this challenging task, coffee and meats danced around in the back of my mind for that whole Christmas holiday month. I decided to let the two ingredients meet, get to know each other, and allow their worlds to mix and flow into a great ballet. A couple of weeks after I returned home from the holiday break, I was full of energy and ideas and went back to my kitchen and usual routine. I was amazed at the wonderful results, and sent samples of my creations all over town. The fact that coffee, with its rough texture and intense flavor, ended up being a great partner with the traditional and sometimes mild savory foods of our table, felt overwhelmingly good. Coffee clings to pan drippings and deepens the flavor of meat sauces, pairs wonderfully with slightly sweet Asian seasonings, and is a welcome addition to reduced balsamic sauces and vinaigrettes.

During my first experiments, I realized several properties about coffee. A surprising one to me is that instant coffee and sugar syrups are not friends. I was stunned at first, as I am one to always sweeten my coffee and assumed the two, along with milk, were pals. Another coffee fact I discovered is that vanilla and cold water are welcome when united with freeze-dried, instant coffee, but definitely *un*welcome with powdered instant coffee. Many days went by as I tried to figure out how to introduce coffee into my favorite foods, and how to incorporate all commercially available forms of coffee into the recipes so that I could offer a range of options for my readers no matter

what type of coffee they have access to. I compared homemade and store-bought espresso, for instance, and both proved to be equally useful. However, as I began to realize that many people cannot make fresh and good espresso at home, I backed away from the idea of it being the main measuring ingredient for all recipes. Powdered instant coffee doesn't hold up to all recipes, either, and neither does regular percolated or drip coffee. So I decided to go to the experts and get some help.

One cold morning I traveled to the hilly, San Francisco–like city of Manizales, Colombia, to meet the head food scientist of the lab of the Colombian Coffee Federation's processing plant. It was a fantastic experience to sit in this huge place where the smell of freshly roasted coffee permeated the air, with a 1,000-square-foot copy of the real plant. This is where all the elaborate testing is done to ensure that only the highest-quality coffee is released to the market every day. The security here is incredible—greater even than the security at the First Lady's office when I brought her my Colombian cookbook as a gift the day before. Right in the middle of the cool air, blue skies, and coffee-covered land of the *Zona Cafetera* in Colombia, we talked about my project and I sat and learned all I could about the extraordinary characteristics of coffee.

We sampled many kinds of mouthwatering coffees and mixtures, and defined their taste, solubility, and many other interesting facts. I discovered that coffee and soda are a delicious combination; another match made in heaven is coffee and vodka. I met the general manager of the plant, and we discussed coffee's many attributes. What most impressed me at the plant was the fact that all the executives—some of the most important people in the country—were not wearing suits and ties. They were dressed in regular clothes and shoes more like the ones a factory worker would wear. They knew everyone and everything that was going on, and they completely loved their work. They have a true passion for coffee. That same day, I traveled back home to Panama with my heart pounding—I was full of energy, ideas, and focus; I needed to continue this wonderful journey with coffee.

Many months went by as I developed more ideas, went through more trial and error with recipes, and developed an even greater intimacy with coffee. I went back to Manizales to learn more about coffee, talked to proud organic and estate coffee growers, and learned about Fair Trade and gourmet-quality coffee. I learned about how the people of this region educate their children who are dispersed throughout small villages in the high mountain ranges. After getting to know so many people in this area and feel the passion in the air for coffee and all that it involves, I decided I would try to interview some of the hardworking pickers and other workers and write the short profiles of their incredible lives that appear earlier in this book.

Coffee is a universally sought-after drink. Many countries have their own ways of preparing it—the popular versions from Turkey, Italy, and Colombia come to mind—and as individuals we have adopted our favorite ways of preparing and drinking it. As a matter of fact, it was in Manizales that I saw my first "barista show," where they demonstrated how to properly prepare the perfect cappuccino: the technique, the machine specs, and more. I learned about the kinds of coffees used for cappuccinos, the correct grinds, the fact that there is less caffeine in an espresso than in a cup of brewed coffee because of the amount of time it is in contact with the hot water, and which Colombian coffees were being used around the world to prepare cappuccinos. It was great to be there in the middle of the Colombian coffee-growing zone learning how to prepare proper Italian cappuccinos!

the individual chapters

I created most of the recipes in this book with freeze-dried coffee (I used the one from the Colombian Coffee Federation). For example, the Concentrated Coffee Syrups are prepared with either freeze-dried or fresh, ground coffee. (I have included three coffee syrup recipes: one for desserts, one for savory foods, and one for drinks.) I have developed different ways of producing the best recipes with the largest variety of coffee types that are available. Many recipes call directly for freeze-dried coffee for ease of preparation. But, for many recipes, you can substitute different coffee types based on the proportions shown in the Basics chapter, with the exception of cookie, biscuit, and biscotti recipes. Some recipes use concentrated coffee or espresso, which I suggest you buy at a coffee store if you do not own a machine; you can just refrigerate it until you are ready to use it.

The first chapter, Basics (pg 22), contains the recipes I developed for many of the essential coffee flavorings that hold together recipes throughout the book. Here you will find delicious caramel sauces, coffee-based syrups, frostings, creams, ganaches, pastries, and more. These coffee basics are responsible for the aroma and essence of coffee

17

in many of the recipes that follow this chapter. They can also be used on their own to highlight other dishes; make some and keep them on hand for regular use.

The next five chapters are mostly dedicated to sweets, with the exception of a few recipes that can be used for sweet or savory dishes, such as the bread loaf, waffles, and biscuits. The Early Birds and Breads chapter (pg 40) contains 16 recipes that can be served for breakfast, brunch, and light dinners. For those of you who host Sunday brunches with kids, you will find ideas such as French Toast with Caramel Coffee Sauce; for a more hearty brunch, add the Banana-Caramel Sauce, the Coffee Belgian Waffles with Yellow Gooseberry Sauce, and sandwiches prepared with the Mocha Sandwich Loaf.

The Bars, Cookies, and Goodies chapter (pg 62) includes cookies that range from the gooey Fantastic Coffee and White Chocolate Chunk Cookies to the Crunchy Oatmeal Coffee Cookies. You will also find Cappuccino Brownies, White Chocolate Mochaccino Bars, Caramel-Coffee Frosted Biscotti, Coconut Coffee Cocadas, a variety of tartlets and truffles, and the airiest, most delicate Ladyfinger Sandwiches. These small treats are all worth trying: they are simple to make, keep well, and are great as after-dinner sweets. I usually cut them or prepare them as miniatures to allow myself multiple tastes.

The Most Moist Cakes (pg 86) are my favorite recipes. I love baking cakes and playing around with different sauces. Some, like the Almond Liquor Coffee Cake, the Coconut Coffee Cake, the Coffee Butter Cake, and the Hot Milk Cake, are easy to make and can even be prepared by children (with adult supervision). The chiffon

cakes and Hot Milk Cake are very versatile and go well with most of the frostings, sauces, and syrups in the book; they can also be served with fruit and cream, ice cream, or simply with powdered sugar. And they are great for entertaining. It's just so nice to have a small piece of homemade cake—it doesn't even have to be frosted—right before bed time or at my favorite time, 4:30 in the afternoon, with…a cup of coffee!

The chapter that I think has the most pizzazz and contains the most extravagant recipes is Cool Desserts (pg 116). Some of the sweets, like the Four Milks Coffee Delight or Mamina's Coffee Mousse, look simple, but they have rich, complex flavors and wonderful sauces. Others are more aesthetically sophisticated (but equally delicious), like the bombes or the Coffee Crème Bavaroise. I also included some everyday desserts like ice cream and the Café Bomba.

The one chapter that could not be missing from a book on coffee recipes is Hot and Cold Drinks (pg 146). From the simplest *tinto*, or black coffee, to the super Ice Cream-Coffee Sundae Party, all of the drinks are a great excuse to drink and eat coffee in new and exciting ways. The most important tip here is to buy the best coffee you can get, and to enjoy it with a friend.

The final chapters were the most difficult for me to begin, but ended up yielding the most wonderful and creative recipes as I realized how well coffee and savory foods match. In some cases, the coffee adds a subtle flavor and richness to the food. In others, the coffee flavor is at the forefront of the dish, yet it highlights the main ingredient and matches it perfectly. People are always pleasantly

surprised when they taste the recipes in the Savory Main Dishes (pg 158) and Greens and More (pg 182) chapters. Try one—maybe the Asian Vinaigrette and a meat like the Lamb Chops with White Balsamic and Yogurt Sauce or the Cornish Game Hens with Berry-Coffee Sauce. You will be completely flabbergasted, I am sure!

I hope you enjoy the recipes in this book as much as I have enjoyed preparing them and giving people the opportunity to experience new and exciting tastes.

kitchen
essentials

First and foremost, you need coffee: freshly ground or freeze-dried instant. Pick your favorite and buy the best. Always keep flour and butter on hand, as well as a can of non-stick cooking oil spray and parchment or waxed paper for your baking; almost all of the baking recipes in the book call for them. Disposable pans and cookie sheets are also good to keep on hand, especially when you plan to give away a batch of brownies, a loaf of bread, or a small cake.

I still place a regular cookie sheet or baking pan under the disposable ones to help me put them into the oven and take them out with out risk of spilling; the regular pans also help to ensure that the bottoms of baked goods are evenly cooked. Another one of my baking tricks is to use flexible, plastic cutting boards for lifting pastry that has stuck to my work table. I put some flour on the edge of one of my boards and gently slide it under all of the pastry, and then I place a tart or pie pan over the pastry and flip it over. It's a great trick that really works!

Other kitchen items I find very useful to have on hand:

- Handheld or stand-up electric mixer

- Immersion or regular blender

- Spatulas—plastic for scraping, metal for decorating

- Pastry bags (20 and 12 inch), couplings, and plain round and star tips

- Rolling pin—one that suits your size (I use a small one)

- Sealable bags, in all sizes (used for storage, as small pastry-decorating bags, and for giving away sweets)

- Inexpensive serrated knife

- Flexible, plastic cutting boards

- Two good oven mitts and a bunch of towels

- Cake pans—I use these most: two heavy, 9-inch cake pans; a large
  Bundt pan; a small (8-inch) and large (10-inch) tube pan; 9-inch and
  10-inch spring form pans

- Cookie sheets—at least 3

- Jelly roll pan

- Baker's half sheets—at least 3

- Muffin pans—2-inch and miniature

- Tart pans—used for pies and quiches in all 3 sizes (4, 9 and 10 inch)

- Loaf pans—9 inch and 10 inch (European size)

- Scoops—very useful, not only for serving ice cream, but for scooping out
  cookie dough and cupcakes evenly; I have the large #24 scoop (cupcakes), a small #40 (mini muffins and cookies), and #60 (smaller cookies)

- Large roasting pan with a nonstick rack

- Small baking pan that fits the toaster oven (with its rack)—this comes in
  handy not only for cookies, but also to cook single or double servings of
  fish or chicken

- Stainless steel bowls—I adore these and have them in all sizes

- Skillets—7 and 11 inch

- Saucepans—in a small, 2-cup size as well as 1 1/2 and 2 1/2 quarts;
  good for melting butter and doing small chores

- 9-quart stock pot—for cooking pasta or preparing stocks

That's basically all you need to stock a usable kitchen.

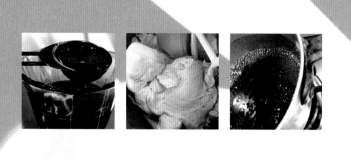

basics

The basic recipes you need to make great desserts are all here—from bases like meringue disks and crêpes, to toppings like rich ganaches, fluffy buttercreams, and airy meringues. Pie doughs in three varieties to create miniature to large sweet and savory tarts and pies. Syrups to carry liqueurs and drench desserts, ice creams, and coffee drinks. Pastry creams to flavor a complete array of extraordinary treats. Delicious sauces to serve with the foods in the book as well as the many desserts, ice creams, sundaes, bread toasts, biscuits, and good foods you can imagine. Try them and keep some in your fridge—they are all prepared with very little effort, and produce a great amount of satisfaction.

Concentrated coffee syrups will be your key to successful coffee cooking throughout this book and with any personal recipes you would love to experiment on. Prepare them and keep them in the fridge; they keep for up to a month if covered well.

The practical tips at the end of this chapter will help you craft these luscious coffee recipes.

balsamic reduction
2 TABLESPOONS REDUCTION

1/4 cup balsamic vinegar

Place the vinegar in a small, heavy nonreactive saucepan and bring to a boil. Lower the heat to a simmer and cook until reduced to 2 tablespoons, or half the original amount. It will look shiny and thick.

basic crêpes
12 6- TO 7-INCH CRÊPES

These basic crêpes are very useful, as they can be transformed into sweet or savory dishes. For savory ones, I usually add 1 tablespoon of chopped cilantro or 2 cilantro sprigs 10 seconds before I turn off the blender. Other times, I add 1/2 teaspoon curry powder or garam marsala instead and serve the crêpes with a chicken and cashew sauce. And, 1/4 teaspoon turmeric yields beautiful, yellow crêpes that go perfectly with a shrimp curry sauce.

1 cup milk
3/4 cup all-purpose flour
1 egg
2 tablespoons butter, melted (plus 2 tablespoons, if using a crêpe pan)
2 teaspoons sugar
1 teaspoon freeze-dried or granulated instant coffee
1/4 teaspoon cinnamon

Electric crepe machine or crêpe pan

1. Place milk, flour, egg, melted butter, sugar, coffee, and cinnamon in a blender. Blend until smooth and let rest for 10 minutes. (This will remove air bubbles.)

2. If using a crêpe machine, follow the manufacturer's instructions. If using a crêpe pan, use the 2 tablespoons of extra melted butter to keep the batter from sticking.

3. If eating on the same day, stack each crêpe on a plate, one on top of the other. When cool, cover with a towel and set aside. If refrigerating for up to 3 days, or freezing for up to a month, place a piece of waxed paper between each crêpe to help them separate when ready to use.

dulce de leche
1 1/4 CUPS (14 OUNCES)

Some of my recipes call for this delicious ingredient that is very popular in Latin America. This quick and easy recipe tastes just as good as traditional versions.

1 14-ounce can condensed milk

Cook the condensed milk in a pressure cooker for 30 minutes. After it cools, it will set and be ready to use.

basic coffee pie dough

2 8- TO 9-INCH CRUSTS
64 2 1/2-INCH ROUNDS FOR 1-INCH TARTLETS

This is a basic coffee-scented pie crust. It works equally well for both sweet and savory dishes, and can be played with by adding extras like ground peppercorns or chopped herbs like dill or sage. For a sweet crust, add cinnamon and allspice or vanilla sugar.

12 tablespoons (1 1/2 sticks) butter
2 1/2 cups all-purpose flour
1 tablespoon sugar
1 tablespoon freeze-dried instant coffee
1/4 teaspoon salt
1/3 cup cold espresso or basic concentrated
   coffee (pg 36)

1. Slice the butter into small pieces and place it in the freezer for 5 minutes.

2. In a food processor, place flour, sugar, instant coffee, and salt, and mix for 3 seconds.

3. Add the frozen butter and process for 10 to 15 seconds more, or until you can no longer see the larger pieces. They will feel like large granules in the flour mixture.

4. Pour in the espresso or concentrated coffee while the processor is on and mix until the ingredients form a dough, and then remove it from the bowl.

5. Shape the dough into a disk, wrap tightly with plastic wrap, and refrigerate for 30 to 45 minutes.

6. Roll the dough to 1/4-inch thickness for an 8- or 9-inch crust, and to 1/8-inch thickness for tartlet shells or disks. (It is easier to roll between two pieces of plastic wrap.)

7. To make a pie crust: place the dough in a pan, gently tamp down and cut off the edges, folding them in to decorate. For small tartlets: cut the dough with a scalloped cookie cutter, set over each small mold, and tamp down gently. For disks: bake cut dough flat on cookie sheets.

8. To bake an empty shell, preheat the oven to 425°F, place foil or paper cups over the dough, fill with beans or weights, and bake until golden and crispy—20 to 25 minutes for larger shells and 12 to 15 minutes for tartlets.

almond pie dough

1 10-INCH PIE CRUST
46 1-INCH MINI TARTLETS

This tasty pie dough can be used for a variety of pies and tarts. You can also use it to make flat, cookie-like rounds and simply place a dollop of cream and a berry on top, serve them with a fruit sorbet, or use them for ice cream sandwiches.

10 tablespoons (1 1/4 sticks) butter
1/4 cup peeled, whole almonds (see tips, pgs 38–39)
1 1/2 cups all-purpose flour
1/4 cup sugar
1/2 teaspoon salt
1 yolk, beaten
1 tablespoon cold water

1. Slice the butter into small pieces and place it in the freezer for 5 minutes.

2. In a food processor, process the almonds and 1/4 cup flour to a fine crumb, about 1 minute. Add the remaining flour, sugar, and salt, and mix for 5 seconds.

3. Add the frozen butter and process for 10 to 15 seconds more, or until you can no longer see the larger pieces. They will feel like large granules in the flour mixture.

4. Pour in the beaten egg yolk and water in a thin stream while the processor is on and mix until the ingredients form a dough, and then remove it from the bowl. If the dough feels too dry, you may need to add an extra 1 to 2 teaspoons of cold water.

5. Shape the dough into a disk, wrap tightly with plastic wrap, and refrigerate for 30 to 45 minutes.

6. Roll the dough to 1/4-inch thickness for an 8- to 10-inch crust, and to 1/8-inch thickness for tartlet shells or disks. (It is easier to roll between two pieces of plastic wrap.)

7. To make a pie crust: place the dough in a pan, gently tamp down and cut off the edges, folding them in to decorate. For small tartlets: cut the dough with a scalloped cookie cutter, set over each small mold, and tamp down gently. For disks: bake cut dough flat on cookie sheets.

8. To bake an empty shell, preheat the oven to 425°F, place foil or paper cups over the dough, fill with beans or weights, and bake until golden and crispy—20 to 25 minutes for larger shells and 12 to 15 minutes for tartlets.

sweet pie dough (*pâte sucrée*)

This sweet pie dough can be used for recipes that call for fillings that are not too sweet, such as yellow gooseberry pie—or even with meat pies, as it adds a hint of sweetness. I love it when my mother makes chicken pie with raisins and olives in this pastry!

12 tablespoons (1 1/2 sticks) butter
2 cups all-purpose flour
1/3 cup sugar
1/2 teaspoon salt
1 egg, beaten
1 to 2 tablespoons cold water, optional

1. Slice the butter into small pieces and place it in the freezer for 5 minutes.

2. In a food processor, place flour, sugar, and salt, and mix for 3 seconds.

3. Add the frozen butter and process for 10 to 15 seconds more, or until you can no longer see the larger pieces. They will feel like large granules in the flour mixture.

4. Pour in the beaten egg while the processor is on and mix until the ingredients form a dough, and then remove it from the bowl. If the dough feels too dry, you may need to add an extra 1 to 2 tablespoons of cold water.

5 Shape the dough into a disk, wrap tightly with plastic wrap, and refrigerate for 30 to 45 minutes,

6. Roll the dough to 1/4-inch thickness for an 8- or 10-inch crust and to 1/8-inch thickness for tartlet shells. (It is easier to roll between two pieces of plastic wrap.)

7. To make a pie crust: place the dough in a pan, gently tamp down and cut off the edges, folding them in to decorate. For small tartlets: cut the dough with a scalloped cookie cutter, set over each small mold, and tamp down gently.

8. To bake an empty shell, preheat the oven to 425°F, place foil or paper cups over the dough, fill with beans or weights, and bake until golden and crispy—20 to 25 minutes for larger shells and 12 to 15 minutes for tartlets.

coffee meringue disks

This meringue is great for all shapes—from cups to ladyfingers.

Butter and nonstick oil spray
5 tablespoons freeze-dried or granulated instant coffee
2 tablespoons water
1 cup egg whites (5 to 6)
3/4 cup granulated sugar
1 1/2 cups powdered sugar

Pastry bag with coupler only or large plain tip

1. Preheat the oven to 220°F.

2. Grease 3 or 4 baking sheets and line them with waxed or parchment paper, or grease the pans and lightly flour them.

3. Mix the coffee and 2 tablespoons of water in a small bowl. Set aside.

4. Beat the egg whites with an electric mixer at medium speed for 1 minute. Increase the speed to high and add the granulated sugar a little at a time until it is completely absorbed and the whites look shiny and stiff, about 4 minutes. Pour the coffee in a thin stream and mix for 1 minute.

5. Turn off the mixer. Add the powdered sugar and mix in for a minimum of 1 minute or until all the sugar has been absorbed.

6. Scoop into large pastry bags with only the plastic coupling or a large plain or star tip.

7. Mark 8-inch rounds (or 2-inch rounds for individual servings) on the buttered paper. Start piping from the center out to create 6 8-inch disks (or 48 2-inch disks).

8. Bake for 1 hour. Set aside to cool. Store in a tin can or box on the paper until ready to use.

TIP: For dry and sturdier meringues, turn off the oven and leave the meringues in until completely dry in the middle, about 30 minutes more or overnight.

coffee whipped cream
ABOUT 2 CUPS WHIPPED CREAM

The cognac flavor is beautifully strong in this cream. If you prefer, you can reduce it to 1/2 tablespoon.

1 cup heavy cream
1/2 cup powdered sugar
2 tablespoons cognac
2 tablespoons concentrated coffee syrup (pg 36)

Place the cream and sugar in a clean, dry mixer bowl. Beat at high speed for 1 1/2 to 2 minutes or until soft peaks form. Add the cognac and coffee syrup and mix to stiff peaks.

almond caramel praline
2 CUPS PRALINE CRUMBS

This praline is so versatile you can use it with every recipe in the book. For extra crunch and sophistication, sprinkle some on anything from waffles to ice cream to frappes. I sometimes add powdered chili, curry powder, or even pepper to play around and give my guests something to talk about at the table!

2 cups sugar
3/4 cup sliced almonds

Nonstick baking sheet

1. Place sugar in a heavy saucepan over medium-high heat. Do not mix until all of it has melted and turned golden yellow, about 7 to 10 minutes. Remove from the heat and mix with a wooden spatula if it gets too dark.

2. While the sugar is cooking, heat a nonstick baking sheet in the oven at 350°F. Remove from the oven when the caramel is ready.

3. Add the almonds to the melted sugar and immediately pour onto the hot pan. Spread with a spatula as thin as you can before it hardens.

4. Set aside to cool, about 10 minutes. Peel off the pan by lifting the whole piece off with the tip of a spatula.

5. To break it into pieces, place pieces into a heavy plastic zipper bag and mash with a meat pounder. Store in airtight containers or sealed plastic bags.

caramelized coffee pecans
2 CUPS PECAN BITS

OH! These have a great flavor. Keep them on hand for unexpected events. Serve them on ice cream with cookies, alongside a hot cappuccino, or as decoration on a cake. They go very far.

1/4 cup light brown sugar
4 tablespoons (1/2 stick) butter
1 teaspoon freeze-dried or granulated instant coffee
1 1/2 cups pecan halves

1. Preheat the oven to 350°F.

2. Combine the sugar, butter, and coffee in a small saucepan. Bring to a boil, then remove from the heat. Add the pecans and mix well to coat.

3. Spread the nuts on a baking sheet and bake for 10 minutes. Remove from the oven, stir with a fork, and set aside to cool for 10 minutes.

4. Keep 8 pecans whole for decoration; process the rest in the food processor for 10 seconds to crush. Store in airtight containers or sealed plastic bags.

spiced caramelized almonds
2/3 CUP ALMONDS

Spiced almonds can be used to add interest to salads, ice creams, and even meats. Keep some in plastic zipper bags in your refrigerator for those unexpected dinners.

1/2 cup sliced almonds
1/4 cup light brown sugar
1/2 teaspoon chili powder
1/2 teaspoon curry powder
1/4 teaspoon cinnamon
2 tablespoons butter, melted

Preheat the oven to 350°F. Place the almonds in a small baking pan. Sprinkle with the sugar and spices, drizzle with melted butter, and mix. Bake for 20 minutes, or until lightly golden. Remove from the oven, stir, and set aside to cool.

dark chocolate ganache
2/3 CUP GANACHE

Use a premium dark chocolate that is at least 60% cacao in this recipe. The ganache can be used to frost, fill, and drizzle over cakes and desserts before it hardens. (It will harden when refrigerated, so keep at room temperature.) This is also a great frosting for brownies. If you prefer sweet chocolate, choose a milk chocolate with around 30% cacao. You can also mix dark and milk chocolates.

4 ounces chocolate
1/4 cup heavy cream

1. Shred or grate the chocolate into a bowl.

2. Place the cream in a small saucepan and bring to a boil; remove immediately from the heat and pour over the chocolate.

3. Mix with a fork until all the chocolate has melted. Refrigerate just until cool and thick enough to cover a dessert.

white chocolate ganache
2/3 CUP GANACHE

The quality of the white chocolate is imperative here. Buy the best and you will see wonderfully delicious results.

5 ounces white chocolate
1/4 cup heavy cream

1. Shred or grate the chocolate and place in a bowl.

2. Place the cream in a small saucepan and bring to a boil; remove immediately from the heat and pour over the chocolate.

3. Mix with a fork until all the chocolate has melted. Refrigerate just until cool and thick enough to cover a dessert.

frostings,
fillings,
and icings

coffee buttercream frosting
2 CUPS FROSTING

This is a very sturdy buttercream. You can also prepare it with the concentrated coffee syrup (pg 36), which makes it just a little softer.

12 tablespoons (1 1/2 sticks) butter
2 1/2 cups powdered sugar
4 tablespoons freeze-dried or granulated instant coffee
1 tablespoon coffee liqueur
1/2 teaspoon vanilla extract
1/4 teaspoon almond extract
1/4 teaspoon salt

Beat the butter with an electric mixer on low speed for 5 minutes, or until you have a creamy mixture. Add the powdered sugar and mix 2 minutes more on low. Combine the coffee, liqueur, extracts, and salt, then add to the butter slowly in a thin stream so it does not curdle. Mix for 2 minutes and set aside.

coffee meringue frosting
3 CUPS FROSTING

The trick to this soft, mouthwatering cream is to bring the syrup to the correct temperature. It is a great frosting to work with—you can use it on jelly rolls and other desserts, or to pipe decorations on cakes. This meringue can also be prepared with the concentrated coffee syrup (pg 36).

3/4 cups sugar
1/3 cup water
1 teaspoon light corn syrup
3/4 teaspoon cream of tartar
1/8 teaspoon salt
2 egg whites
1 tablespoons freeze-dried or granulated instant coffee (plain)
1 tablespoon coffee liqueur or concentrated coffee syrup (pg 36)
1/2 teaspoon vanilla extract
1/4 teaspoon almond extract

1. Combine the sugar, water, corn syrup, cream of tartar, and salt in a small saucepan over medium-high heat. Bring to a boil and cook until it reaches 250°F.

2. Place the whites in a clean mixer bowl and whip at medium-high speed for 2 minutes, until stiff peaks form. Add the sugar syrup in a thin stream until completely absorbed, about 2 minutes. Continue mixing for 3 minutes.

3. Combine instant coffee and extracts, add coffee liqueur or concentrated coffee syrup, and pour into the whites mixture. Mix for 2 minutes.

4. Set aside until ready to use.

TIP: If the meringue sits for over an hour, turn the machine on and mix again on high for 1 to 2 minutes, or until shiny and thick again. If using flavored instant coffee, such as vanilla or macadamia, add an extra 1 teaspoon coffee.

29

basics

coffee pastry cream
2 CUPS CREAM

Beautiful, shiny, and a dark caramel color, this cream can used to fill tarts topped with fresh fruit, between sheets of flaky pastry in *millefeuilles* (napoleons), and as a frosting for chiffon cakes and jelly rolls.

2 cups whole milk
3/4 cup granulated sugar
4 egg yolks
3 tablespoons cornstarch
6 tablespoons espresso or concentrated coffee
   syrup (pg 36)
2 teaspoons vanilla sugar (see tips, pgs 38–39)
1/8 teaspoon salt

Whisk or handheld mixer

1. Combine the milk, sugar, egg yolks, cornstarch, espresso or coffee syrup, vanilla sugar, and salt in a medium saucepan. Mix well with a whisk or handheld mixer.

2. Place over medium heat, mixing continuously until the mixture thickens, about 8 to 10 minutes.

3. Pass through a sieve into a shallow pan. Cover with waxed paper. Refrigerate until set, at least 1/2 hour, or overnight.

cream cheese–coffee buttercream frosting I
2 CUPS FROSTING

4 tablespoons (1/2 stick) butter
4 ounces cream cheese
1 1/2 cups powdered sugar
1 1/2 tablespoons amaretto-flavored freeze-dried
   or granulated instant coffee
1 tablespoon amaretto
1/2 teaspoon vanilla extract
1/4 teaspoon almond extract
1/4 teaspoon salt

1. Beat the butter and cream cheese with an electric mixer on low speed for 5 minutes or until creamy. Add the powdered sugar and mix 2 minutes more.

2. Combine the coffee, amaretto, extracts, and salt. Add to the mixture slowly in a thin stream so the butter does not curdle. Mix for 2 minutes and set aside.

cream cheese–coffee buttercream frosting II
2 CUPS FROSTING

This is very sweet but more sturdy than the first version.

4 tablespoons (1/2 stick) butter
4 ounces cream cheese
2 1/2 cups powdered sugar
2 tablespoons freeze-dried or granulated instant coffee
2 tablespoons concentrated coffee syrup (pg 36)
   or coffee liqueur
1/4 teaspoon salt

1. Beat the butter and cream cheese with an electric mixer on low speed for 5 minutes or until creamy. Add the powdered sugar and mix 2 minutes more.

2. Combine the coffee syrup or liqueur, extracts, and salt. Add to the mixture slowly in a thin stream so the butter does not curdle. Mix for 2 minutes and set aside.

dry coffee icing
2/3 CUP FROSTING

This is a perfect frosting for cupcakes, buns, biscotti, and sweets—especially when you plan to carry them in a container. It dries up and doesn't stick! Keep it refrigerated in plastic zipper bags. Just open the bag and mix back to softness with a small spoon or fork and transfer to a new bag (leaving the dried pieces in the old bag). Voilà!

1 cup powdered sugar, sifted (see tips, pgs 38–39)
2 tablespoons coffee liqueur
1 tablespoons freeze-dried or granulated instant coffee
1 to 1 1/2 tablespoons water

1. Place 1/2 cup of the powdered sugar in a small bowl. Add the liqueur, coffee, and 1 tablespoon water and mix with a fork until smooth.

2. Add the remaining sugar and mix again. If you feel you need the extra tablespoon water to get to the right consistency, add it and mix well.

TIP: If you want to make the frosting ahead of time, just cover it with plastic wrap and leave at room temperature.

espresso buttercream frosting
1 HEFTY CUP FROSTING

This buttercream is very easy to prepare and is great when you need only a small amount of frosting, such as for the coconut coffee cake (pg 000). You can also use it on cupcakes or cookies.

8 tablespoons (1 stick) butter
1 1/2 cups powdered sugar
3 tablespoons brewed espresso or basic concentrated coffee (pg 36)
1/2 teaspoon almond extract

1. Beat the butter with an electric mixer on low speed for 2 minutes, or until it has a creamy texture. Add the powdered sugar and mix 2 minutes more.

2. Add the espresso or coffee slowly in a thin stream so the butter does not curdle.

3. Add the extract, mix 2 minutes more, and set aside until ready to use.

mocha buttercream frosting
2 CUPS FROSTING

8 tablespoons (1 stick) butter
3 tablespoon cocoa powder
2 cups powdered sugar
3 tablespoons brewed espresso or basic concentrated coffee (pg 36)

1. Beat the butter with an electric mixer on low speed for 5 minutes, or until it has a creamy texture.

2. Combine the cocoa and powdered sugar, and slowly add to the butter. Mix 2 minutes more. Add the espresso or coffee slowly in a thin stream so the butter does not curdle. Set aside until ready to use.

fluffy coffee buttercream frosting
2 CUPS FROSTING

This fluffy frosting is great for all types of desserts. It's very important to bring the sugar syrup to the right temperature or something magical might happen: the frosting could disappear the next day!

6 tablespoons (3/4 stick) butter
1 1/4 cups powdered sugar
1 tablespoons freeze-dried or granulated instant coffee
1 tablespoon coffee liqueur or water
1/2 teaspoon vanilla extract
1/4 teaspoon almond extract
1/2 cup granulated sugar
1/4 cup water
1 teaspoon light corn syrup
1 egg white
1/4 teaspoon cream of tartar
1/8 teaspoon salt

1. Beat the butter with an electric mixer on low speed for 5 minutes, or until it has a creamy texture. Add the powdered sugar and mix on low 2 minutes more. Combine the coffee, liqueur or water, and extracts, and slowly add to the butter in a thin stream so that it does not curdle. Mix for 2 minutes and set aside.

2. Combine the granulated sugar, water, and corn syrup in a medium saucepan. Bring to a boil and continue cooking until it reaches 250°F.

3. Place the egg white in a clean mixer bowl. Add the cream of tartar and salt. Mix with clean beaters at medium-high speed for 2 minutes.

4. Add the hot sugar syrup mixture one tablespoon at a time until completely absorbed, about 2 minutes. Continue mixing for 3 minutes. Fold the butter mixture in with soft circular motions.

5. Refrigerate until ready to use.

31

basics

balsamic reduction sauce
3 TO 4 TABLESPOONS SAUCE

This reduced balsamic can be kept refrigerated for up to a week. Use it to enhance many dishes—even sweets, such as coffee ice cream with berries or mangoes.

1/4 cup balsamic vinegar
2 teaspoons heavy cream
2 tablespoons brown sugar
1 teaspoon freeze-dried instant coffee
1/2 teaspoon water

1. Place the vinegar in a small, heavy nonreactive saucepan, bring to a boil, lower the heat to simmer, and cook until reduced to 2 tablespoons or half the original amount. It will look shiny and thick.

2. Place cream and brown sugar in a small saucepan and cook over low heat to dissolve. Remove from heat.

3. In a small container, combine coffee and water. Add to the cream and brown sugar mixture. Add the reduced vinegar and mix well.

4. Set aside until ready to use.

bananas in coffee-caramel sauce
1 1/3 CUPS SAUCE

You can use this sauce with ice cream, waffles, pancakes, and even yogurt!

2 firm bananas
1 tablespoon butter
1 teaspoon ground cinnamon
Pinch nutmeg
1/3 cup firmly packed dark brown sugar
3 tablespoons brewed espresso, or 3 tablespoons brewed regular coffee
   plus 1 teaspoon freeze-dried or granulated instant coffee
1 tablespoon coffee liqueur
1/3 cup heavy cream

1. Peel and cut the bananas into 1/4-inch slices, about 1 3/4 cups slices.

2. In a sauté pan over medium heat, combine the butter, cinnamon, and nutmeg. Allow the butter to melt and bring out the flavor of the spices, about 1 minute.

3. Add the sugar, espresso or coffee mix, and liqueur and cook 3 to 5 minutes, until the sugar has melted and the mixture has started to boil.

4. Add the cream and simmer until golden, about 2 minutes. Add the bananas and cook 1 minute more.

5. Keep warm until ready to use.

caramel coffee sauce
1/2 CUP SAUCE

This is the best sauce in the book! It brings out the best in anything you add it to and takes only seconds to prepare.

1/4 cup firmly packed dark brown sugar
1/4 cup heavy cream
3 tablespoons brewed espresso or basic concentrated coffee (pg 36)
1 tablespoon butter

Combine the sugar, cream, and coffee in a small saucepan. Bring to a boil and cook for 30 seconds to 1 minute, mixing continuously. Turn off the heat, mix in the butter, and set aside to cool.

caramel coffee sauce with macadamia or amaretto
1/2 CUP SAUCE

1/4 cup firmly packed dark brown sugar
5 tablespoons heavy cream
1 1/2 tablespoons macadamia or amaretto-flavored freeze-dried or granulated instant coffee
2 tablespoons butter

Combine the sugar, cream, and coffee in a saucepan. Bring to a boil and cook for 30 seconds to 1 minute, mixing continuously. Turn off the heat, mix in the butter, and set aside to cool.

coffee crème anglaise sauce
1 1/2 CUPS SAUCE

1 1/2 cups milk
1/2 cup firmly packed dark brown sugar
1/4 cup heavy cream
3 egg yolks
2 teaspoons vanilla sugar (see tips, pgs 38–39)
1/8 teaspoon salt
3 tablespoons concentrated coffee syrup (pg 36)

Place the milk, brown sugar, cream, egg yolks, vanilla sugar, and salt in a blender. Blend just to combine and transfer to a heavy saucepan. Bring to a boil and cook over medium-low heat, mixing continuously until thickened, about 8 minutes. Add the coffee syrup and mix well. Cool.

cranberry sauce I
1/2 CUP SAUCE

This sauce goes well with pancakes, waffles, and ice creams.

1/4 cup evaporated milk
1/4 cup heavy cream
3 tablespoons light brown sugar
3 tablespoons chopped, toasted pecans (see tips, pgs 38–39)
2 tablespoons cranberries, dried
1 tablespoons brewed espresso or basic concentrated coffee (pg 36)
1/2 teaspoon vanilla extract

Combine the evaporated milk, cream, sugar, pecans, and cranberries in a saucepan over medium heat. Bring to a boil and simmer for 4 to 5 minutes, until golden. Add the coffee and vanilla extract and stir to blend. Serve warm.

cranberry sauce II
3/4 CUP SAUCE

This sauce keeps for more than two weeks when refrigerated.

1/2 cup heavy cream
6 tablespoons light brown sugar
6 tablespoons slivered almonds
6 tablespoons cranberries, dried
2 tablespoons freeze-dried or granulated instant coffee
1 teaspoon vanilla extract

Combine the cream, sugar, pecans, cranberries, coffee, and vanilla extract in a saucepan over medium heat. Cook for 2 to 3 minutes or until golden. Serve warm.

33

mocha-rum sauce
3/4 CUP SAUCE

1/2 cup coffee beans
1/3 cup powdered sugar
1 1/2 tablespoons butter
2 tablespoons dark rum
1 cup heavy cream
1 teaspoon vanilla extract
1/2 ounce chocolate, shaved (see tips, 38–39)

1. Place coffee beans in a food processor and pulse briefly to chop only to a consistency that you can later strain out.

2. Place the chopped beans, sugar, and butter in a sauté pan and cook over medium heat for 3 minutes, or until the butter has melted.

3. Add the rum and continue to cook until well mixed, about 1 minute. Reduce the heat if necessary, so that the mixture doesn't burn.

4. Stir in the cream and bring to a simmer, cook for 1 minute more and remove from the heat. Stir in the vanilla and pass the mixture through a strainer. Add the chocolate and stir until dissolved. Discard the solids.

5. Covered with waxed paper and refrigerate.

TIP: You can omit the chocolate for a delicious coffee-rum sauce.

rum coffee cream sauce
SCANT 1 CUP SAUCE

1/2 cup heavy cream
2/3 cup powdered sugar
3 tablespoons brewed espresso
1 tablespoon dark, aged rum
1/2 tablespoon cornstarch

Place all ingredients into a small saucepan and mix well. Stirring slowly but constantly, bring to a boil over medium-low heat and cook for 3 minutes. Cool.

dark chocolate sauce
1 CUP SAUCE

A super-simple and delicious chocolate sauce that can be served over ice cream, cookies, chiffon cakes, or anything you dream of covering in chocolate.

1/4 cup whole milk
1/4 cup heavy cream
1/4 cup sugar
4 ounces dark chocolate, finely chopped

Combine the milk, cream, and sugar in a small saucepan and bring to a boil. Immediately remove from the heat and pour over the chocolate. Mix with a fork until all of the chocolate has melted. Refrigerate until cool and thickened.

passion fruit sauce I
1 CUP SAUCE

The mint and ginger give this delicious sauce a unique flavor. It can also be transformed into a sauce for seafood just by adding a little salt, pepper, and spice. This sauce can be refrigerated for up to a week and reheated.

1/2 cup passion fruit pulp (see tips, pgs 38–39)
1/4 cup water
1/2 cup sugar
1 tablespoon cornstarch
10 mint leaves, whole
1 teaspoon minced pickled ginger

1. In a small saucepan, combine the pulp, water, sugar, cornstarch, and mint leaves.

2. Bring to a boil. Cook until the sauce has thickened, about 5 to 7 minutes. Turn off the heat.

3. Add the ginger, mix, and set aside for 5 minutes.

passion fruit sauce II
SCANT 1 CUP SAUCE

This is a lighter version of passion fruit sauce that can be used for more intricate dishes or for everyday morning toast. It can be refrigerated for up to a week.

1 tablespoon flour
1 tablespoon butter, softened
5 tablespoons passion fruit pulp (see tips, pg 38–39)
1/2 cup water
1/2 cup tablespoons sugar
1 teaspoon grated orange zest

1. In a small bowl, mix flour and butter with a fork to form a paste. Transfer to a small saucepan.

2. Mix in the pulp, water, and sugar. Bring to a boil and cook until the sauce has thickened, about 5 to 7 minutes.

3. Turn off the heat. Add the zest, mix well, and set aside for 5 minutes.

white chocolate–coffee sauce
SCANT 1 CUP SAUCE

5 ounces white chocolate
2 tablespoons milk
4 tablespoons heavy cream
2 tablespoons concentrated coffee syrup (pg 36)
1 tablespoon coffee liqueur

1. Shred or grate the white chocolate into a bowl.

2. Heat the milk and cream in a saucepan over medium heat until the mixture begins to boil. Turn off and pour over the white chocolate.

3. Mix with a fork until smooth. Stir in the coffee syrup and liqueur, and set aside.

yellow gooseberry sauce
3/4 CUP SAUCE

This is a tangy, full-bodied sauce that can be spooned over buttery slices of warm bread, chiffon cakes, pancakes, French toast, or ice cream. It can be refrigerated for more than 2 weeks.

1 1/2 cups yellow gooseberries (divided use)
1/3 cup sugar
1 teaspoon lime juice
1 1/2 teaspoons cornstarch
1 tablespoon butter

1. Combine 1 cup gooseberries with sugar, lime juice, and cornstarch in a small saucepan. Cook over medium heat, stirring constantly, for 4 to 6 minutes or until it boils and thickens.

2. Remove from heat, add the butter, and mix until dissolved. Set aside to cool.

3. Cut the remaining 1/2 cup of gooseberries into quarters. When the sauce is cool, add the cut-up gooseberries. Mix gently with a fork.

basic simple syrup
1/2 CUP SYRUP

This light syrup can be used to preserve the flavor of liquors and extracts in cakes and desserts when they would otherwise evaporate in the baking process. It is very versatile—you can prepare it with herbs, such as mint and basil; with fruit to make fruit sorbets or smoothies; or with liqueurs to pour over ice creamsand fresh fruit.

1/2 cup water
1/3 cup sugar

Place sugar and water in a small saucepan. Bring to a boil until the sugar dissolves. Turn off the heat and set aside to cool.

VARIATIONS: To prepare with herbs: combine 3/4 cup water with 20 mint leaves. To prepare with spices: combine 3/4 cup water with 2 star anise, 1/4 teaspoon cinnamon, and 1/4 teaspoon allspice. Microwave either preparation on high for 1 1/2 minutes. Remove, cover, and set aside for 3 to 5 minutes. Blend, pass through a fine sieve, and measure 1/2 cup to use in recipe above.

coffee syrups

I developed these syrups for many different uses: basic concentrated coffee is an all-purpose flavoring, the concentrated coffee syrup is mainly for sweets, sweet coffee syrup is for drinks, and savory coffee syrup is a sauce that can be used with meats and vegetables. These syrups can be prepared with freshly ground coffee or freeze-dried, granulated instant coffee.

basic concentrated coffee (unsweetened)
1 CUP CONCENTRATED COFFEE

In a regular drip coffee maker, use 1 1/2 cups freshly ground, high-quality coffee and 2 cups water. Run the coffee maker to yield 1 cup of strong coffee. The coffee can be refrigerated and used instead of espresso.

concentrated coffee syrup I (with freeze-dried coffee)
1/2 CUP SYRUP

1/2 cup sugar
1/2 cup freeze-dried or granulated instant coffee
1/4 cup water

1. Place sugar, coffee, and water in a small saucepan and mix well. Bring to a simmer over medium heat. Reduce the heat to medium-low and cook for 3 to 5 minutes, or until thickened and reduced to 1/2 cup.

2. Pass through a strainer or remove residue with a spoon. Set aside to cool. Refrigerate.

concentrated coffee syrup II
(with ground coffee)
2/3 CUP SYRUP

1 1/2 cups freshly ground coffee
2 cups water
1/2 cup sugar

1. In a coffee maker, brew the ground coffee with all of the water.

2. Place the brewed coffee in a tall saucepan (coffee boils high) with the sugar and bring to a boil. Reduce the heat to medium and cook for 10 to 12 minutes or until reduced to a thick syrup. Set aside to cool. Refrigerate.

sweet coffee syrup for drinks I
(with freeze-dried coffee)
SCANT 1 CUP SYRUP

6 tablespoons freeze-dried or granulated instant coffee
3/4 cup granulated sugar
2 tablespoons dark brown sugar
3/4 cup water
1 tablespoon light corn syrup

In a heavy saucepan, mix the coffee, sugars, water, and corn syrup. Place over medium-high heat and bring to a boil. Let it simmer about 5 minutes or until thickened and shiny. Set aside to cool. Refrigerate.

sweet coffee syrup for drinks II
(with ground coffee)
1 CUP SYRUP

1 1/4 cups freshly ground coffee
1 2/3 cups water
3/4 cup granulated sugar
2 tablespoons dark brown sugar
1 tablespoon light corn syrup

1. In a coffee maker, brew the ground coffee with all of the water.

2. Place the brewed coffee in a tall saucepan (coffee boils high) with the sugars and corn syrup and bring to a boil. Reduce the heat to medium and cook for 10 to 12 minutes or until reduced to a thick syrup. Set aside to cool. Refrigerate.

savory coffee syrup I
(with freeze-dried coffee)
SCANT 1 CUP

1/4 cup freeze-dried or granulated instant coffee
1/4 cup water
1/2 cup granulated sugar
1/4 cup dark brown sugar
2 tablespoons tomato paste
1 tablespoon balsamic vinegar
1/4 teaspoon freshly ground black pepper

In a saucepan, combine the coffee, water, sugars, tomato paste, vinegar, and pepper. Bring to a boil over medium heat, about 3 minutes. Simmer for 2 to 3 minutes more, or until shiny and thickened. Set aside to cool. Refrigerate.

savory coffee syrup II (with ground coffee)
SCANT 1 CUP

3/4 cups ground coffee
1 cup water
3/4 cup granulated sugar
1/4 cup dark brown sugar
2 tablespoons tomato paste
1 tablespoon balsamic vinegar
1/4 teaspoon freshly ground black pepper

1. In a coffee maker, brew the ground coffee with all of the water.

2. Place the brewed coffee in a small saucepan with sugars, tomato paste, vinegar, and pepper. Bring to a boil, reduce the heat, and simmer for 10 to 12 minutes, or until reduced to 1 cup and thickened. Set aside to cool. Refrigerate.

chocolate leaves: Pick some leaves from your garden in a size and shape that you like. Wash and dry them well. Melt couverture chocolate in the microwave on high for 45 to 50 seconds. Mix with a fork and brush onto clean leaves. Make sure you do not let the chocolate go over the edges or it will stick and the leaves will break. Refrigerate or set aside in a cool place for 5 minutes, or until they have hardened enough to peel. Without applying pressure to the chocolate, peel the real leaf away. Refrigerate chocolate leaves until ready to use.

clarifying butter: Melt the butter in a saucepan, remove the white solids from the top, pass through a cheese cloth, and freeze until solid. For a "trick of the trade" simpler process: Melt the butter in a sauce pan, transfer to a bowl, and freeze until solid. Pass a knife around the sides, remove the solid block of clarified butter, and discard the liquids left over in the bowl.

coffee substitutions: In most of the recipes you can substitute 1 tablespoon of freeze-dried coffee for 2 tablespoons of basic concentrated coffee (pg 36) prepared with a ratio of 3 tablespoons ground coffee to 4 tablespoons water. You can also substitute 1 tablespoon of freeze-dried coffee with 1 tablespoon concentrated coffee syrup (pg 36).

flambéing: Igniting the alcohol in a dish or sauce, which burns off the alcohol but leaves the flavor of the liqueur. Often done for visual presentation, the process actually changes the chemistry, and therefore the flavor, of the food. To flambé, carefully add the liqueur to the sauce while the pan is not over heat. Return the pan to heat and slant it just until the alcohol reaches the flame. You may also use a long fireplace match. **CAUTION:** Do not carry the dish while flaming and keep a large metal lid on hand in case the flame gets out of control. Keep away from the flame and keep hair pulled back or covered.

flour substitution (for cornstarch in sauces): Use double the quantity of flour as cornstarch called for in the recipe. Make a paste of equal amounts of flour and softened butter (for example, 1 tablespoon flour and 1 tablespoon butter). Place the paste in the saucepan with the other sauce ingredients over medium-high heat and stir for 7 to 8 minutes, or until the sauce has thickened and no longer tastes like flour.

julienned basil leaves: Make a small stack of leaves, one on top of the other, roll into a log, and slice thinly.

nonreactive containers: Nonreactive containers are those made of materials that will not react with acids, such as stainless steel, glass, and plastic. Reactive materials, such as aluminum, will cause unpleasant changes in the appearance and flavor of some ingredients.

passion fruit pulp: Cut a heavy passion fruit in half and spoon the seeds and juice into a sieve set over a bowl. With the spoon, mix and press lightly until only the seeds and white covering are left in the sieve; discard these. In the bowl under the sieve is the pulp with pure fruit juice for the recipe. Do not add water or blend, or you will be left with vanilla seed–like black dots.

pastry bag substitution: If you do not have a pastry (decorating) bag, use a plastic zipper bag with the corner cut off. Use a tiny snip for a drizzle, or a larger cut for a larger amount.

puréed yellow gooseberries: When puréeing yellow gooseberries, they do not need to be passed through a sieve. The seeds are very small, and it is okay to leave them.

peeled almonds: Place almonds in a small saucepan, cover with water, and bring to a boil.

Cook until the skins blow up, about 2 minutes, and strain. Set over a piece of cloth and rub until the skins come off.

rehydrating raisins: Place raisins in water overnight. Or, heat raisins in water over medium-high heat for a couple of minutes. They will absorb the liquid and plump up.

seasoning and marinating: Place meats in plastic zipper bags and refrigerate. Overnight marination is best for large pieces of beef and pork, or whole chickens. For smaller amounts of beef, pork, and chicken, 1 hour will do. For seafood, 15 minutes is enough. In fact, if left overnight with an acidic ingredient such as lime juice or vinegar, seafood will "cook."

shaving—chocolate or parmesan: Run a potato peeler along the edge of a block of an ingredient such as high-

quality chocolate or parmesan cheese. Use the best you can find of these ingredients.

sifting: Do not sift flour or powdered sugar unless directed. Place flour or powdered sugar in a bowl and mix with a fork before measuring. For powdered sugar: 1/3 cup unsifted is equal to about 1/2 cup sifted.

tamarind preparation: From pods: remove the seeds and pulp and discard the pods. Press the pulp through a sieve. From packages of seeds and pulp: place in a saucepan with 4 times the amount of water, and cook over medium-low heat to extract all the pulp. Pass through a sieve with a spoon or fork to remove as much pulp from the seeds as possible. From packages of thick pulp: place in a saucepan and add twice the amount of water. Simmer until completely dissolved.

thickened yogurt: Place yogurt in a coffee filter over a strainer, with a bowl under the strainer. Allow it to sit overnight in the refrigerator, or for 3 to 4 hours on the kitchen counter. It will have the consistency of sour cream.

toasting—almonds, coconut, pecans, and pine nuts: Place ingredient on a baking pan in a preheated oven, until golden and aromatic. For almonds and pecans, heat at 350°F for 8 to 10 minutes. For coconut shavings, heat at 425°F for 10 minutes. For pine nuts, heat at 350°F for 3 to 4 minutes.

toasting—spice seeds: Place spice seeds, such as cumin or anise, in a sauté pan over low heat and swirl the seeds until you can smell their aroma. Grind in a clean coffee or spice grinder, or by hand with a mortar and pestle. Preparing the spices this way creates an intense aroma, yet will yield a more rounded and subtle flavor. This gives you more control over a recipe's taste, since preground spices can vary with different brands and product age.

vanilla sugar: Scrape out the seeds of a split vanilla bean, then rinse and dry it. Grind the bean in a clean coffee grinder or spice mill with 1 cup sugar.

early birds
and breads

This is actually the first chapter I started working on. I always make waffles (and other "early bird" foods) at home for Sunday breakfast, so this was my preferred starting point. Also, people tend to think of coffee as a breakfast drink, though nowadays it is being served with other meals more often than when I was a child in the early 1960s.

This chapter includes a range of versatile recipes—from coffee waffles and pancakes to the mocha sandwich loaf to biscuits and buns. Eat the mocha loaf by itself, or use it to make out-of-this-world french toast. And enjoy the biscuits, probably my favorite recipe in this chapter, with ham and cheese, eggs and cheese, or a drizzle of caramel coffee sauce.

These are very straightforward recipes, so you can indulge yourself at any time. The breads take a little longer to make, but are worth it. (If you have the time, you can also prepare the breads with a "sponge," which will add even more flavor; see the tip on the last page of this chapter.) Enjoy these goodies with friends and family and have fun making them!

chocolate-dotted waffles

with caramel coffee sauce

Dreamy waffles for those with a child's sweet tooth. These traditional, thin waffles can be frozen and then sealed in plastic bags for daily use. Just pop them frozen into a toaster, and you are ready to go.

1 3/4 cups all-purpose flour
2 tablespoons freeze-dried or granulated instant coffee
2 ounces dark chocolate shavings
6 tablespoons granulated sugar
1 teaspoon baking powder
1/2 teaspoon baking soda
1/4 teaspoon salt
3 eggs
1 1/4 cups buttermilk or yogurt
4 tablespoons (1/2 stick) butter, melted
1 teaspoon vanilla extract
1/4 teaspoon almond extract
1 pint vanilla ice cream or whipped cream
1 recipe caramel coffee sauce (pg 33)
Powdered sugar, optional

Regular waffle maker

1. Place the flour, coffee, chocolate, granulated sugar, baking powder, baking soda, and salt into a large bowl. Mix with a fork.

2. In another bowl, mix the eggs, buttermilk or yogurt, butter, and extracts. Add this to the flour mixture and mix gently with a fork until the batter looks smooth.

3. Spray the waffle maker with nonstick spray and place 1/3 of the mixture on the surface of the machine. Cook until set, about 2 to 3 minutes. Repeat with remaining batter.

4. Serve the waffles warm, topped with ice cream or whipped cream and caramel sauce. Sprinkle with powdered sugar, if desired.

coffee belgian waffles

with caramel coffee sauce

This thick European street food is a Sunday tradition at my house. Serve them with ice cream and caramel sauce, or just with powdered sugar—both ways are fantastic. They are also great with yellow gooseberry sauce (pg 35).

7 4-INCH WAFFLES

1 1/2 cups all-purpose flour
5 tablespoons granulated sugar
1 teaspoon baking powder
1/2 teaspoon baking soda
1/4 teaspoon salt
3 tablespoons freeze-dried or granulated instant coffee (divided use)
3 eggs
1 1/4 cups buttermilk or yogurt
4 tablespoons (1/2 stick) butter, melted
1 teaspoon vanilla extract
1 pint coffee ice cream or whipped cream
1 recipe caramel coffee sauce (pg 33)
2 tablespoons powdered sugar

Belgian waffle maker

1. Place the flour, granulated sugar, baking powder, baking soda, salt, and 2 tablespoons of the coffee into a medium bowl. Mix with a fork.

2. In another bowl, thoroughly mix the remaining 1 tablespoon coffee, eggs, buttermilk or yogurt, butter, and vanilla.

3. Pour into the dry ingredients and gently combine with a fork until you can no longer see any flour. Do not overmix.

4. Spray the waffle maker with nonstick spray and place 1/3 cup of the batter on the surface. Cook until set, 2 to 3 minutes. Repeat with the remaining batter.

5. Serve the waffles warm, topped with ice cream or whipped cream and caramel sauce. Sprinkle with powdered sugar.

egg-white coffee belgian waffles

with yellow gooseberry sauce and mango

These egg-white waffles are a great alternative for those on restricted diets. But they are also great when you are left with egg whites and don't know what to do with them. No one will notice notice that anything is missing!

4 4-INCH WAFFLES

1 ripe mango, peeled and sliced
3 1/2 tablespoons granulated sugar (divided use)
1 recipe yellow gooseberry sauce (pg 35)
3/4 cup all-purpose flour
1 1/2 tablespoons freeze-dried or granulated instant coffee (divided use)
1/2 teaspoon baking powder
1/4 teaspoon baking soda
1/8 teaspoon salt
3/4 cup buttermilk or yogurt
3 tablespoons oil
1/2 teaspoon vanilla extract
3 egg whites
2 tablespoons powdered sugar

Belgian waffle maker

1. Preheat the broiler. Lay mango slices on broiler pan, spray them lightly with cooking spray, sprinkle with 1 tablespoon of the granulated sugar, and broil for 5 minutes. Add them to the yellow gooseberry sauce and set aside.

2. Place the remaining 2 1/2 tablespoons of sugar, flour, 1 tablespoon of the coffee, baking powder, baking soda, and salt into a medium bowl. Mix with a fork.

3. In another bowl, thoroughly mix the remaining 1/2 tablespoon coffee, buttermilk, oil, and vanilla.

4. Pour into the dry ingredients and gently combine with the fork until you can no longer see flour. Do not overmix.

5. In a large bowl, beat the whites to soft peaks—with a wire whisk, about 2 minutes; with an electric mixer, about 1 minute. Add some of the whites to the batter and then fold all of the batter into the rest of the whites.

6. Spray the waffle maker with nonstick spray and place 1/3 cup batter on the surface. Cook until set, 2 to 3 minutes. Repeat with the remaining batter. (They might take a little longer than regular waffles to set.)

7. Serve the waffles warm with mango-gooseberry sauce and powdered sugar.

all-whites mocha waffles
with passion fruit sauce

These waffles are a nice breakfast for a special occasion, as well as for tea or brunch. The passion fruit sauce can be kept refrigerated for a week and used on toast or biscuits.

16 4-INCH WAFFLES

1 1/2 cups all-purpose flour
6 tablespoons granulated sugar
1 tablespoon unsweetened cocoa
1 teaspoon baking powder
1/2 teaspoon baking soda
1/4 teaspoon salt
2 tablespoons freeze-dried or granulated instant coffee
1 teaspoon vanilla extract
1/4 teaspoon almond extract
1 1/4 cups buttermilk or yogurt
6 tablespoons oil
6 egg whites
1 recipe passion fruit sauce (pg 34)
1 pint passion fruit sorbet
2 tablespoons powdered sugar

Regular waffle maker

1. Place the flour, granulated sugar, cocoa, baking powder, baking soda, and salt into a bowl. Mix with a fork.

2. In another bowl, thoroughly mix the coffee and extracts. Add the buttermilk or yogurt and oil, and mix thoroughly. Pour into the flour mixture and gently combine with a fork until you can no longer see flour.

3. In another bowl, beat the whites to soft peaks—with a wire whisk, about 2 minutes; with an electric mixer, about 1 minute. Add some of the whites to the batter, then fold all of the batter into the rest of the whites.

4. Spray the waffle maker with nonstick spray and place 1/3 cup of the batter on the surface. Cook until set, about 2 to 3 minutes. Repeat with the remaining mixture. (They might take a little longer than regular waffles to set.)

5. Serve the waffles warm, topped with the passion fruit sauce and passion fruit sorbet. Sprinkle with powdered sugar.

coffee oatmeal pancakes

with bananas in coffee-caramel sauce

Morning miniatures with a huge flavor.
Delicious, healthy, and energizing.

1/2 cup plus 2 tablespoons all-purpose flour
1/4 cup raw oatmeal (rolled oats)
2 tablespoons raisins, finely chopped
1 tablespoon brown sugar
1 teaspoon baking powder
1/2 teaspoon ground cinnamon
1/4 teaspoon salt
1 teaspoon freeze-dried or granulated instant coffee
6 tablespoons milk
1 egg
1 tablespoon butter, melted
1 recipe bananas in coffee-caramel sauce (pg 32)
1 tablespoon powdered sugar

1. Place flour, oatmeal, raisins, brown sugar, baking powder, cinnamon, and salt into a small bowl. Mix with a fork.

2. In a separate bowl, add the coffee to the milk and mix. Pour into the flour mixture. Add the egg and butter. Mix gently with a fork until the dry ingredients have been moistened.

3. Place a 6-inch nonstick pan over medium-low heat. Spray with nonstick spray.

4. Pour 1/3 cup of batter into the pan and cook until golden brown, about 1 to 1 1/2 minutes. Turn and cook for 20 seconds more, until golden on the second side. (The second side takes less time.)

5. Serve pancakes warm, topped with the bananas and sauce. Sprinkle with powdered sugar.

coffee whole-wheat pancakes

with cranberry sauce

A healthy and great way to introduce whole wheat into your diet. The whole family will love them.

3/4 cup whole-wheat flour
2 tablespoons dried cranberries
2 tablespoons light brown sugar
1 teaspoon freeze-dried or granulated instant coffee
1 teaspoon baking powder
1/4 teaspoon salt
1 1/2 tablespoons butter, melted
1 egg
1/2 cup milk
1 recipe cranberry sauce (pg 33)

1. Place the flour, cranberries, brown sugar, coffee, baking powder, and salt into a small bowl. Mix with a fork.

2. Add the butter, egg, and milk and mix gently with a fork until the batter looks smooth.

3. Place a 6-inch nonstick pan over medium-low heat. Spray with nonstick spray.

4. Pour 1/4 cup of batter into the pan and cook until golden brown, about 1 to 1 1/2 minutes. Turn and cook for 20 seconds more, until golden on the second side. (The second side takes less time.)

5. Serve pancakes warm, topped with the cranberry sauce.

47

egg-white french toast

with yellow gooseberry sauce

This great French toast is perfect for those who can only eat egg whites. Remember to buy bread that does not have eggs in it.

2 egg whites

1/4 cup milk

2 tablespoons brewed espresso or 3/4 teaspoon freeze-dried or granulated instant coffee mixed with 2 tablespoons brewed regular coffee

2 teaspoons granulated sugar

1/4 teaspoon salt

2 large slices whole-wheat bread (1/2 inch thick)

6 tablespoons (1/2 recipe) yellow gooseberry sauce (pg 35)

2 tablespoons powdered sugar

1. Beat the egg whites with the milk, coffee, granulated sugar, and salt to a soft, foamy texture in a shallow dish. Place the bread slices in the mixture, let sit for 30 seconds, turn over, and let sit until ready to cook.

2. Spray a large sauté pan with nonstick spray. Place over medium heat and add the bread slices. Decrease the heat to medium-low and cook for 2 minutes, until lightly golden.

3. Turn the bread and cook on the other side for 1 minute more, until lightly golden. Remove from the pan and set on a plate.

4. Serve warm with yellow gooseberry sauce and powdered sugar.

with caramel coffee sauce

I love this recipe, and with the mocha sandwich loaf it is absolutely out of this world. If you don't have time to make the mocha sandwich loaf, find a large cinnamon or mocha bread loaf in a good bakery to enjoy the full sensation.

2 SERVINGS

2 eggs
2 tablespoons milk
6 tablespoons coffee liqueur (divided use)
1/2 teaspoon salt
4 1/2-inch-thick slices mocha sandwich loaf (pg 53)
1/2 teaspoon butter
1/4 cup sliced almonds
1/4 cup light brown sugar
1/4 cup water

1. Beat the eggs with the milk, 2 tablespoons of the liqueur, and the salt in a shallow dish. Place the bread slices in the mixture, let it sit for 30 seconds, turn over, and let sit until ready to cook.

2. Spray a large sauté pan with nonstick spray and add the butter. Place over medium heat, let the butter melt, and add the bread. Decrease the heat to medium-low and cook for 2 minutes, until lightly golden.

3. Sprinkle the almonds over the bread and around the pan. Turn the bread slices and cook on the other side for 1 minute more or until lightly golden. Remove from the pan and set on a plate.

4. Add the sugar, the remaining liqueur, and water to the pan and simmer for 1 to 2 minutes. Drizzle over the slices.

banana–coffee pudding cups

More delicious than pretty, these are a nutritious breakfast for a long work day. Serve them with a fruit cup and work as you eat. Cinnamon bread works great with this recipe.

2 eggs
1/2 cup milk
1/4 teaspoon salt
1/8 teaspoon freshly ground black pepper
Pinch ground nutmeg
4 slices bread (3, if the slices are thick), diced into 1/2-inch cubes
1/4 cup sliced almonds, toasted
1 recipe bananas in coffee-caramel sauce (pg 32), room temperature
2 tablespoons powdered sugar

Muffin tin with 2 1/2-inch cups

1. Preheat the oven to 425°F. Spray or butter eight 2 1/2-inch muffin cups, then lightly flour them.

2. Beat the eggs with the milk, salt, pepper, and nutmeg in a shallow dish. Add the bread cubes to the mixture and let them soak completely, about 2 minutes.

3. Add almonds and half of the bananas in coffee-caramel sauce. Mix with a spatula.

4. Spoon the mixture into each muffin cup. (This is easily done with an ice cream scoop). Bake for 25 to 30 minutes, until set. Allow to stand for 5 minutes. Pass a knife around the sides to loosen and remove each cup. Place onto serving plates.

5. Spoon the remaining bananas in coffee-caramel sauce over the puddings and sprinkle with powdered sugar.

biscuits

1 1/2 cups all-purpose flour
3 tablespoons sugar
2 teaspoons baking powder
1/2 teaspoon ground cinnamon
1/2 teaspoon salt
8 tablespoons (1 stick) unsalted butter, chilled and sliced
3/4 cup heavy cream
1 1/2 teaspoon freeze-dried or granulated instant coffee
Butter and jam or *dulce de leche* (pg 24)

1. Preheat the oven to 450°F. Butter and flour an 8-inch cake pan.

2. Mix the flour, sugar, baking powder, cinnamon, and salt in a food processor for 5 seconds.

3. Add the butter pieces and process to fine crumbs, about 15 seconds.

4. Mix the cream and coffee and pour into the processor. Mix until a dough forms and separates from the sides of the processor, about 15 seconds.

5. Use an ice cream scoop to place 1/3-cup scoops of the dough onto the pan. Bake for 20 to 25 minutes.

6. Serve with butter and jam or *dulce de leche* for spreading.

The best biscuits in the world—you could add chocolate chips, blueberries, dried cranberries, or white raisins to create a variety for a brunch or breakfast buffet. You can freeze the biscuits right after they come out of the oven. When you're ready to eat them, defrost overnight and reheat in a toaster oven.

sandwich loaf

1 cup water
1 tablespoon instant dry yeast
1 tablespoon honey
4 cups all-purpose flour (divided use)
1/4 cup sugar
1 tablespoon cocoa
1 teaspoon salt
2 tablespoons freeze-dried or granulated instant coffee
2 tablespoons milk
1 egg
1/4 cup oil
1/4 teaspoon almond extract
2 teaspoons ground coffee beans
2 teaspoons sugar
2 tablespoons butter, melted

1. In a glass measuring cup, warm the water in the microwave for 30 seconds, or until it feels warm to the touch but does not burn (about 110°F). Add the yeast and honey, cover, and set aside for 10 minutes.

2. Mix 3 1/2 cups flour, sugar, cocoa, and salt in a food processor for 5 seconds.

3. In a small bowl, dissolve the instant coffee in the milk, then mix in the egg, oil, and extract. Add to the flour mixture in the processor. Then pour the yeast mixture into the processor and mix for 30 seconds.

4. Add the remaining 1/2 cup flour to the processor and mix for 10 seconds more, or until a dough forms and separates from the bowl.

5. Coat a large bowl with nonstick spray. Transfer the dough to the bowl and cover with a towel. Set aside in the warmest, draft-free part of your kitchen for 1 hour and 15 minutes, or until doubled in size.

6. Transfer to a floured work counter, and roll or spread with your hands to a 12 × 8-inch rectangle. Mix the ground coffee beans and sugar. Brush the dough with butter and sprinkle with sugar and coffee mixture. Roll like a jelly roll, transfer to a buttered and floured 12 × 6-inch loaf pan. Cover again and let rise for another hour. During the second rising, preheat the oven to 350°F.

7. Bake for 45 minutes or until golden. Set aside to cool for 10 minutes and slice. (An electric knife works wonders here.)

This unique sandwich bread has a light texture and delicate flavor, and it's easy to prepare at home. Slice it with an electric knife and store it in a plastic zipper bag for convenience. You can freeze it sliced in case you want to save it for special occasions.

53

early
birds
and
breads

divine

coffee

rolls

1/2 cup water
1 tablespoon instant dry yeast
1 tablespoon honey
4 cups all-purpose flour (divided use)
1/3 cup granulated sugar
1 teaspoon salt
2 eggs (divided use)
1/2 cup milk
4 tablespoons (1/2 stick) butter, melted
1/4 cup freeze-dried or granulated instant coffee (divided use)
1/2 teaspoon almond extract
2 tablespoons coffee liqueur
1/2 cup pecans
1/2 cup (packed) light brown sugar
1/3 cup (1/2 recipe) dry coffee icing (pg 30)

2 8-inch cake pans or 2 12-cup (2 1/2-inch) muffin pans

An all-time favorite, and worth the time. If you like, you can freeze part of the dough in the baking pan after half of the second rising, and thaw it in the refrigerator overnight when you're ready to use it. Then bake and allow your home to be filled with all the aroma of these extraordinary rolls.

1. In a glass measuring cup, warm the water in the microwave for 30 seconds, or until it feels warm to the touch but does not burn (about 110°F). Add the yeast and honey, cover, and set aside for 10 minutes.

2. Mix 3 1/2 cups of the flour, granulated sugar, and salt in a food processor for 5 seconds.

3. Mix one egg, milk, butter, 2 tablespoons of the coffee, and extract in a small bowl. Add to the flour mixture in the processor. Then pour the yeast mixture into the processor and mix for 30 seconds.

4. Add the remaining 1/2 cup of flour to the processor and mix for 10 seconds, or until a dough forms and separates from the bowl.

5. Coat a large bowl with nonstick spray. Transfer the dough to the bowl and cover with a towel. Set aside in the warmest, draft-free part of your kitchen for 1 hour and 20 minutes, or until doubled in size.

6. In a small bowl, mix the remaining coffee and the liqueur. Chop the pecans in the food processor with 10 pulses and set aside.

7. Transfer the dough to a floured work counter and roll or spread with your hands to a 24 x 6-inch rectangle.

8. Beat the remaining egg, and brush the dough with about half of the beaten egg. Sprinkle with 3/4 of the brown sugar and pecans, then drizzle with the coffee mixture. Roll like a jelly roll and cut into 1 1/3-inch slices.

9. If using cake pans, butter them, line with parchment paper, and butter and flour the paper and sides; if using muffin pans, butter and flour 18 of the cups. Transfer the rolls to the pans (9 rolls to each cake pan).

10. Sprinkle with the remaining sugar and pecans. Cover again and let rise for another hour. Preheat the oven to 325°F.

11. Bake for 20 minutes or until lightly golden. Remove from the oven and immediately scrape the sides of the pans with a knife or spatula and remove the rolls onto a large platter.

12. Drizzle the frosting over the buns using a pastry bag or a plastic bag (see tips, pg 38–39).

13. Serve warm or set aside at room temperature. Do not refrigerate.

pizza sticks
with coffee drizzles

Fun food like this keeps kids interested. Get together and let them help once you are at the last rising of the bread. It's fun and easy to spread this soft and manageable dough.

30 7 × 3/4-INCH STICKS

1 cup water
1 tablespoon instant dry yeast
1/3 cup plus 1 1/2 tablespoons granulated sugar (divided use)
2 3/4 cups all-purpose flour (divided use)
3/4 teaspoon salt
3 tablespoons oil
1 tablespoon milk
1 tablespoon freeze-dried or granulated instant coffee
2 teaspoons ground coffee beans
1 tablespoon oil or melted butter
1/3 recipe rum coffee cream sauce (pg 34)
1/2 recipe caramel coffee sauce (pg 33)

1. In a glass measuring cup, warm the water in the microwave for 30 seconds, or until it feels warm to the touch but does not burn (about 110°F). Add the yeast and 1/2 teaspoon sugar, cover, and set aside for 10 minutes.

2. Mix 2 1/2 cups flour, 1/3 cup sugar, and salt in a food processor for 5 seconds.

3. Combine the oil, milk, and instant coffee in a small bowl. Add to the flour mixture in the processor. Then pour the yeast mixture into the processor and mix for 30 seconds.

4. Add the remaining 1/4 cup of flour to the processor and mix for 10 seconds more, or until a soft dough forms and separates from the bowl.

5. Coat a large bowl with nonstick spray. Transfer the dough to the bowl and cover with a towel. Set aside in the warmest, draft-free part of your kitchen for 1 hour and 15 minutes, or until doubled in size.

6. Spray your fingertips with oil and use them to remove the dough from the bowl. Transfer it to an 11 × 15-inch baking sheet and spread it with your fingertips.

7. Cover again and let rise for another hour. Preheat the oven to 425°F. Bake for 12 to 15 minutes or until golden.

8. Mix the ground coffee beans with the remaining 4 teaspoons sugar. Brush the dough with oil or butter and sprinkle with the ground coffee mixture.

9. Cut in half to yield 2 rectangles that are about 5 × 7-inches. Slice each one into 3/4-inch-wide strips.

10. To serve warm, place the sauces in separate pastry bags or plastic bags (see tips, pg 38–39). Drizzle the cream sauce diagonally over the slices. Drizzle the caramel sauce in the opposite direction.

11. To serve later, store sticks in plastic zipper bags and then toast them to reheat. Drizzle the sauces after reheating.

sweet coffee loaf (pan dulce)

This sweet, special bread can be served as a snack on its own. A twist on traditional bread, this bread comes out of the oven with holes on the inside and a great caramel flavor. Line the pan with waxed paper to prevent it from sticking. I bet you will eat the whole thing right out of the oven without ever cutting it!

1/2 cup water
1 tablespoon instant dry yeast
1 tablespoon honey
4 cups all-purpose flour (divided use)
3/4 cup granulated sugar (divided use)
1 teaspoon salt
1 egg
1/2 cup milk
1/4 cup oil
2 tablespoons freeze-dried or granulated instant coffee
1/2 teaspoon almond extract
2 teaspoons ground coffee beans
2 tablespoons butter, melted
1/2 cup sliced almonds

1. In a glass measuring cup, warm the water in the microwave for 30 seconds, or until it feels warm to the touch but does not burn (about 110°F). Add the yeast and honey, cover, and set aside for 10 minutes.

2. Mix 3 1/2 cups flour, 1/2 cup sugar, and salt in a food processor for 5 seconds.

3. Combine the egg, milk, oil, instant coffee, and extract in a small bowl. Add to the flour mixture in the processor. Then pour the yeast mixture into the processor and mix for 30 seconds.

4. Add the remaining 1/2 cup of flour to the processor and and mix for 10 seconds more, or until a dough forms and separates from the bowl.

5. Coat a large bowl with nonstick spray. Transfer the dough to the bowl and cover with a towel. Set aside in the warmest, draft-free part of your kitchen for 1 1/2 hours, or until doubled in size.

6. Lightly coat the inside of a 12 × 6-inch loaf pan with butter, and line the pan with waxed or parchment paper. Butter the paper and sprinkle lightly with flour.

7. Transfer the dough to a floured work counter and roll or spread with your hands to a 12 × 8-inch rectangle.

8. Mix the ground coffee beans and the remaining 1/4 cup sugar. Brush the dough with butter and sprinkle it with the coffee mixture and almonds. Roll like a jelly roll, and press the sides and ends to seal.

9. Transfer to the prepared pan. Cover again and let rise for another hour. Preheat the oven to 350°F.

10. Bake for 45 minutes or until golden. Set aside to cool for 10 minutes and slice into 3/4- to 1-inch-thick slices. (An electric knife works wonders here.)

57

early birds and breads

surprise buns

Trébol means "cloverleaf" in Spanish, and is a symbol of luck and surprise. The surprise bean in the center of each bun brings out the coffee flavor of the whole bread.

18 2-INCH BUNS

2 tablespoons water
1 tablespoon instant dry yeast
1 cup plus 1/4 teaspoon granulated sugar (divided use)
2 3/4 cups all-purpose flour (divided use)
1 teaspoon salt
1 egg
3/4 cup milk
1 cup melted butter (2 sticks) (divided use)
4 tablespoons freeze-dried or granulated instant coffee
1 recipe caramel coffee sauce (page 33)
18 whole roasted coffee beans
Granulated sugar for sprinkling

2 12-cup (2 1/2-inch) muffin pans
Pastry bag with #7 round tip

1. In a glass measuring cup, warm the water in the microwave for 5 seconds, or until it feels warm to the touch but does not burn (about 110°F). Add the yeast and 1/4 teaspoon sugar, cover, and set aside for 10 minutes.

2. Mix 2 1/2 cups flour, the remaining 1 cup sugar, and salt in a food processor for 5 seconds.

3. Combine the egg, milk, 1/2 cup of the butter, and instant coffee in a small bowl. Add to the flour mixture in the processor. Then pour the yeast mixture into the processor and mix for 30 seconds.

4. Add the remaining 1/4 cup of flour to the processor and mix for 10 seconds more, or until a soft dough forms and separates from the bowl.

5. Coat a large bowl with nonstick spray. Transfer the dough to the bowl and cover with a towel. Set aside in the warmest, draft-free part of your kitchen for 1 hour and 15 minutes, or until doubled in size.

6. Place the caramel coffee sauce in a pastry bag fitted with a # 7 round tip and set aside. Lightly spray 18 of the muffin cups with nonstick spray.

7. Transfer the dough to a floured work counter and roll into an 18 × 1 1/2-inch rope. Cut into 18 pieces, then cut each of these into 3 pieces.

8. Roll each piece into a ball and fill each one with a little of the sauce by inserting the tip of the tube into the dough and pressing lightly. Dip them in the remaining melted butter and place 3 in each of the oiled muffin cups. Cover again and let rise for another hour. Preheat the oven to 350°F.

9. Sprinkle the buns with sugar and place a coffee bean in the center of each bun. Bake for 20 to 25 minutes or until golden.

10. Remove from the oven, and set aside to cool for 10 minutes. Serve warm.

apple and coffee

crêpe purses

This beautiful and simple recipe can be served at brunch or dinner. Prepare them ahead of time and keep them refrigerated, covered with a damp towel and plastic wrap. Then just heat them up to warm the filling and brown the tops of the crêpe purses.

1/2 cup whole peeled almonds (see tips, pgs 38–39)
3 tablespoons granulated sugar
2 tablespoons heavy cream
1 tablespoon butter
2 large green apples, peeled and diced
1 teaspoon freeze-dried or granulated instant coffee
1/2 teaspoon ground cinnamon
1/4 teaspoon salt
10 to 12 basic crêpes (pg 24)
caramel coffee sauce (pg 33)

Kitchen twine, optional

1. Place the almonds and sugar in a food processor and grind to a powder, about 2 minutes. Add the cream and process to a ball, about 20 seconds more. Set aside.

2. Melt the butter in a sauté pan, add the apples, and sprinkle with coffee, cinnamon, and salt. Mix and cook over medium heat for 3 to 5 minutes, or until the apples start to soften. Remove from heat and set aside.

3. Place the crêpes, one at a time, on a plate or sheet pan. Add a tablespoon of the almond and apple mixture to each. Bring the sides up and close at the top like little purses. Press the centers together so they hold. If they open up, tie them with kitchen twine which you can remove later. Cover until ready to use.

4. Preheat the oven to 425°F. Bake the crêpe purses for 4 to 5 minutes, until the tops of the are golden. Serve with the caramel coffee sauce.

Making a sponge (prefermentation) first will give your yeast breads extra flavor! Try this with any of the bread recipes in this chapter.

KEEP ON HAND:

Butter and flour for your work counter and pan
Nonstick cooking oil spray
Waxed or parchment paper

DAY 1

1. Combine all of the liquids in the recipe and let come to room temperature in a large bowl. Add an equal volume of flour (from the total in the recipe) and a pinch of yeast. Mix by hand until it forms a slurry.

2. Set aside at room temperature for 30 minutes to 1 hour, then cover and refrigerate for 24 hours.

DAY 2

3. Remove the bowl from the refrigerator and let the slurry come to room temperature.

4. Combine the remaining flour and all of the other dry ingredients (including the full measure of yeast) and mix them in a food processor for 2 seconds.

5. Add the slurry and all other ingredients to the processor and mix for 30 seconds, or until the dough forms a ball, then mix for 10 seconds more.

6. Remove the dough from the processor bowl, place in a large oiled bowl, cover, and let it rise in a warm, draft-free place for about 1 hour.

7. Punch down the dough and form it into the desired shape or place it into a pan. Allow for a second rise of 1 hour or more.

8. Bake according to the recipe.

bars, cookies, and goodies

This chapter contains recipes for all of the sweets you dreamed of as a child: cookies, brownies, tarts, and bars. But these treats delight grown-ups as well. The colorful fruit tartlets, coffee-spiked biscotti, and luscious ladyfinger sandwiches will dress up your buffet table or liven any business meeting. And many of these sweets are practical—truffles and coffee balls, for instance, can be prepared ahead of time and kept frozen or refrigerated in sealed bags, ready to bring out for unexpected guests or special occasions.

I have made dozens of cookies from these recipes for tasting panels that included children, teenagers, and adults, all of whom keep asking me for more!

biscotti

8 tablespoons (1 stick) unsalted butter
3/4 cup sugar
2 cups all-purpose flour
1 teaspoon baking powder
1/2 teaspoon baking soda
1/4 teaspoon salt
2 tablespoons freeze-dried or granulated instant coffee
2 tablespoons milk
1/2 teaspoon almond extract
2 eggs
1/2 cup walnut pieces
1 recipe dry coffee icing (pg 30)

Biscotti and coffee are a match made in heaven. These are very easy to make and keep for weeks in tins. Keep some on hand and you will always have a delicious snack.

1. Preheat the oven to 350°F. Lightly butter or spray nonstick oil on a baking sheet.

2. Cream the butter and sugar with an electric mixer at medium speed for 3 to 5 minutes, until fluffy.

3. In a separate bowl, mix the flour, baking powder, baking soda, and salt with a fork. Combine the coffee, milk, and almond extract in another bowl.

4. Turn the mixer to low. Add 1 egg and mix until completely incorporated. Add the other egg and mix for 1 minute. Add the flour mixture and mix for 1 minute. Add the coffee mixture and mix for 30 seconds. Add the walnuts and mix for 1 minute.

5. Divide the dough in half. Place one half on a buttered baking sheet and shape it into a 12 × 3-inch log, then flatten it to 3/4-inch thick (the final size will be about 12 × 4 × 3/4 inches). Do the same with the other half on another baking sheet.

6. Bake each for 20 to 25 minutes or until lightly golden. Remove from the oven and set aside for 10 minutes. Lower the oven temperature to 325°F.

9. Cut each log into slices 1/2-inch thick. Lay the slices flat on the baking sheets. Return to the oven for 25 minutes more or until completely dry.

10. Cool completely on a rack. Dip half of each biscotti into the icing and set on waxed paper to dry.

cappuccino brownies

The easiest recipe in the book! For those who want to get it right the first time, I suggest making this delight. After cuttting the brownies, you can freeze them, unfrosted, in the pan if desired. Then serve them to unannounced guests alone or topped with ice cream, caramel coffee sauce, or just powdered sugar.

12 2 1/2 × 3-INCH BROWNIES

4 ounces unsweetened chocolate
10 tablespoons (1 1/4 sticks) butter
3 eggs
2 tablespoons concentrated coffee syrup (pgs 36–37) or brewed espresso
1 teaspoon vanilla extract
2 1/2 cups sugar
1 cup all-purpose flour
1/4 teaspoon salt
Powdered sugar, optional
1 recipe mocha buttercream frosting (pg 31), optional
1 recipe coffee whipped cream (pg 27), optional

1. Preheat the oven to 350°F. Butter and flour a 12 × 7 1/2 × 2-inch baking pan.

2. Place the chocolate and butter in a glass bowl and microwave on high for 1 minute. Mix with a fork until evenly blended.

3. Mix the eggs, coffee syrup, and vanilla extract in a medium bowl and set aside.

4. Combine the sugar, flour, and salt in a large bowl. Add the chocolate and egg mixtures to the bowl and mix with a fork or spatula.

5. Pour batter into the prepared pan and bake for 45 minutes. Set aside to cool completely in the pan.

6. If desired, sprinkle with powdered sugar or frost with a thin layer of mocha buttercream frosting before serving.

7. Cut and serve the individual brownies. Top with whipped cream flowers, if desired.

coffee
chocolate chip cookies

These large cookies can also be formed with a small ice cream scoop. You can freeze the unbaked scoops in plastic zipper bags, and bake when desired.

24 COOKIES

8 tablespoons (1 stick) butter
2/3 cup firmly packed dark brown sugar
1/4 cup granulated sugar
1 egg
1 teaspoon vanilla extract
1 1/2 cups all-purpose flour
1 1/2 tablespoons freeze-dried instant coffee
1/2 teaspoon baking soda
1/4 teaspoon salt
1 cup chocolate chips (6 ounces)
2 tablespoons concentrated coffee syrup (pgs 36–37)

1. Preheat the oven to 375°F. Line 2 baking sheets with waxed or parchment paper, and spray with nonstick spray.

2. Beat the butter and sugars in an electric mixer on low speed for 3 minutes.

3. Add the egg and vanilla extract, and mix for 2 minutes more.

4. In a medium bowl, mix the flour, coffee, baking soda, and salt with a fork.

5. Add the flour mixture to the mixer bowl and mix for 30 seconds.

6. Add the chips and coffee syrup and mix 30 seconds more.

7. Scoop out 2 tablespoons of dough at a time and set 12 scoops on each baking sheet.

8. Bake for 12 to 15 minutes, until the top surface looks dry. Remove from the oven and set aside.

9. When the baking sheet is cool, peel the cookies off the paper and set on a rack. When they cool completely, store them in covered tins.

VARIATION: You can substitute 3 tablespoons brewed espresso for the instant coffee. Mix the espresso with the egg in step 3, and add 2 extra tablespoons of flour in step 4.

crispy speckled white

chocolate chip coffee cookies

Interesting freckled cookies—just like me! The second addition of coffee does not melt in the batter, and the cookies come out speckled. This is good cookie for a bake sale or a buffet.

36 2-INCH COOKIES

8 tablespoons (1 stick) butter
1 cup sugar
1 egg
2 1/2 tablespoons vanilla-flavored freeze-dried instant coffee (divided use)
1/2 teaspoon vanilla extract
1 1/2 cups all-purpose flour
1/2 teaspoon baking soda
1/4 teaspoon salt
1 heaping cup white chocolate chips

1. Preheat the oven to 300°F. Line 3 baking sheets with waxed or parchment paper, and spray with nonstick spray.

2. Beat the butter and sugar in an electric mixer on low speed for 3 minutes.

3. Mix the egg, 1 tablespoon of the coffee, and the vanilla extract in a small bowl. Add to the mixer bowl, and mix for 2 minutes more.

4. In a medium bowl, mix the flour, remaining instant coffee, baking soda, and salt with a fork.

5. Add to the mixer bowl and mix for 10 seconds. Add the chips and mix for 10 seconds more.

6. Scoop out 2 tablespoons of dough at a time and set 12 scoops on each baking sheet.

7. Bake for 20 to 25 minutes, until the edges look slightly browned. Remove from the oven and set aside.

8. When the baking sheet is cool, peel the cookies off the paper and set on a rack. When they cool completely, store them in covered tins.

divine
coffee
butter
cookies

Beautiful little tea cookies. For sandwiches, fill with the mocha buttercream frosting (pg 31) or any of the other frostings, but only when you are ready to serve them.

80 1-INCH COOKIES OR 40 SANDWICHES

1/2 pound clarified butter (see tips, pgs 38–39)
3/4 cup powdered sugar
1/2 teaspoon vanilla extract
2 cups all-purpose flour
2 tablespoons freeze-dried or granulated instant coffee

1. Preheat the oven to 325°F. Lightly spray 2 or more baking sheets with nonstick spray.

2. Beat the butter in an electric mixer on medium speed for 2 minutes.

3. Sift the powdered sugar into the mixer bowl, and continue to mix for 8 to 10 minutes. Mix in the vanilla extract.

4. In a medium bowl, mix the flour and coffee. Reduce speed to low and add to the mixer bowl. Beat only to incorporate, no more than 1 minute. It will be a dry, textured dough.

5. Scoop out 1 tablespoon portions (easier to do with a small ice cream scoop). Cut each portion in half, roll into balls, place on the baking sheets, and flatten with your hand.

6. Bake for 15 to 20 minutes, until lightly golden. Set aside to cool, about 5 to 10 minutes.

7. Store in covered tins or containers for up to a week.

dulce
de leche
and coffee
squares

This is the sweetest dessert on Earth. It has the crunch of the pecans, the softness of the *dulce de leche*, and the fluffiness of the beaten whites. Try it, and indulge yourself to the max.

16 2-INCH SQUARES

8 tablespoons (1 stick) butter
3/4 cup sugar (divided use)
2 eggs, separated
2 cups all-purpose flour
1/3 cup finely chopped pecans (10 pulses in the food processor)
1/4 cup *dulce de leche* (pg 24)
1 tablespoon freeze-dried or granulated instant coffee
2 teaspoons water
2 teaspoons concentrated coffee syrup (pgs 36–37)
1/4 teaspoon cream of tartar
Pinch of salt

1. Preheat the oven to 350°F. Lightly butter an 8 × 8-inch baking pan, or spray with nonstick oil.

2. Mix the butter and 1/4 cup of the sugar in an electric mixer at medium-low speed for 10 minutes, until it looks light and fluffy.

3. Add the egg yolks one at a time, until each one is completely absorbed. Add the flour and pecans and mix for 1 minute more, or just until incorporated. The batter will be thick.

4. Scrape the batter into the pan. Smooth the top with a spatula for an even crust. Prick the whole surface with a fork.

5. Bake for 15 to 20 minutes, until lightly golden. Remove the crust from the oven and let cool for 10 minutes. (Do not turn off the oven.)

6. Mix the coffee and water. Add the coffee syrup and *dulce de leche*, and mix to a smooth and spreadable consistency. Spread mixture on top of the cooled crust.

7. Place the egg whites in a clean mixer bowl. Add the cream of tartar and salt, and beat at medium-high speed for 1 minute. When the whites are foamy, add the remaining sugar 1 tablespoon at a time, beating until you have a stiff meringue.

8. Spread the meringue on top, and bake for 20 minutes more. The meringue will have set and dried up.

9. Cool and cut into squares. It is okay for the meringue to crack when you cut it.

fantastic coffee

and white chocolate chunk cookies

These cookies are quickly gobbled up whenever I send them to school with my daughters. They never even make it past the first class period! I usually prepare them late in the evening when my girls remember that they promised to bring them.

36 COOKIES

8 tablespoons (1 stick) butter
1 cup sugar
1 egg
1/2 teaspoon vanilla extract
1 1/2 cups all-purpose flour
1/4 teaspoon baking soda
1/4 teaspoon salt
1 1/2 cups white chocolate chunks
1/4 cup brewed espresso or 2 tablespoons freeze-dried instant coffee dissolved in 3 tablespoons water

1. Preheat the oven to 350°F. Line 3 baking sheets with waxed or parchment paper, and spray with nonstick cooking spray.

2. Beat the butter and sugar in an electric mixer on low speed for 3 minutes. Add the egg and vanilla extract and mix for 2 minutes more.

3. In a medium bowl, mix the flour, baking soda, and salt with a fork. Add to the mixer bowl and mix for 30 seconds.

4. Add the chocolate chunks and coffee and mix for 30 seconds more.

5. Scoop out 2 tablespoons of dough at a time and set 12 scoops on each baking sheet. Refrigerate for 5 to 10 minutes.

6. Bake for 15 to 17 minutes, until lightly golden. Remove from the oven and set aside.

7. When the baking sheet is cool, peel the cookies off the paper and set on a rack. When they cool completely, store them in covered tins.

bars,
cookies,
and
goodies

ladyfingers

5 eggs, separated
2/3 cup granulated sugar (divided use)
1 teaspoon vanilla extract
1 cup all-purpose flour
1/2 teaspoon grated orange zest
1/8 teaspoon cream of tartar
1/8 teaspoon salt
2 tablespoons freeze-dried or granulated instant coffee
1 tablespoon powdered sugar

Pastry bag with 3/4-inch plain round tip

1. Preheat the oven to 350°F. Grease 2 baking sheets and line with waxed or parchment paper or lightly flour the pans.

2. Mix the egg yolks, 2 tablespoons of the granulated sugar, and the vanilla extract in an electric mixer at medium-low speed for 2 to 3 minutes, until shiny. Add the flour and orange zest, and mix for 15 to 20 seconds or until just absorbed. Set aside.

3. In a clean bowl, place the egg whites, cream of tartar, and salt. Beat at medium-high speed until frothy, about 1 minute. Add the remaining granulated sugar, and mix on high speed for 8 minutes, until shiny and thick.

4. Fold the whites mixture into the yolk mixture. Fold in the coffee.

5. Pour into a large #20 pastry bag with a round 3/4-inch tip. Pipe out 3-inch logs of batter 1/2 inch apart on each pan. Sprinkle with the powdered sugar.

6. Bake for 18 to 20 minutes, until the cookies spring back and feel sturdy when you touch them, or until the sides and tops are golden.

7. Remove from the oven and place onto a rack to cool completely. Peel from the paper when completely cold or the next day. Store in airtight containers or sealed bags.

These ladyfingers can be eaten alone, with caramel sauce, buttercream frostings, chocolate ganache, or many other fillings and sauces in the book. Add some extra powdered sugar, if desired. Or, if the filling you will be using is very sweet, top with powdered instant coffee. They are delicious any way you eat them!

ladyfinger
sandwiches

Delicate, beautiful, and perfect for grand occasions.

1 cup (1/2 recipe) coffee pastry cream (pg 30)
1 recipe caramel coffee sauce (pg 33) or powdered sugar
1 recipe ladyfingers (pg 72)

Pastry bag with 3/4-inch plain round tip

1. Refrigerate the pastry cream until set. Pour into a large #20 pastry bag with a round 3/4-inch tip. (You can also spread the cream on with a spatula.)

2. Place 18 ladyfingers flat side up on a serving dish or pan. Top each with cream, and cover with another ladyfinger, flat side down.

3. Drizzle some caramel sauce over each sandwich or sprinkle with powdered sugar.

73

bars,
cookies,
and
goodies

oooh!
pecan
phyllo
bites

A crunchy, gooey, yet not-too-sweet little bar that is much easier to prepare than it seems.

1 cup caramelized coffee pecans (pg 28)
4 ounces cream cheese
2 1/2 tablespoons sugar
1 teaspoon freeze-dried instant coffee
10 phyllo sheets, thawed overnight in the refrigerator if frozen
4 tablespoons (1/2 stick) butter, melted

1. Preheat the oven to 350°F. Line a baking sheet with waxed or parchment paper, and butter or spray with nonstick oil.

2. Set aside 39 caramelized pecan halves. Place the remainder of the pecans into a food processor and grind for 7 seconds, or 3 pulses.

3. In a small bowl, mix the cream cheese, sugar, and coffee with a fork. Stir in the ground pecans.

4. Keep the phyllo sheets covered with a damp towel as you work. Place a sheet of phyllo on a work surface and softly brush with butter. Do this for 7 sheets total, stacking them one on top of the other.

5. Place 1/3 of the ground pecan mixture along one end of the longer side of the sheet and another 1/3 on the opposite end. Roll each end to the center, creating two rolls side by side. Cut the phyllo down the center to separate the two rolls, and cover them with a damp towel.

6. Butter and stack the 3 remaining phyllo sheets, cut in half lengthwise and place the halves on top of each other, making a stack of 6 narrow sheets. Spread the remaining ground pecan mixture on the long side and roll. (You will have 3 long rolls altogether.)

7. Cut each roll into 13 pieces. Place each piece on the baking sheet, seam side down. Brush with melted butter and place a caramelized pecan on top of each one.

8. Bake for 35 to 45 minutes, until golden and crispy throughout.

white chocolate

mochaccino bars

These brownie-like bars are fantastic to keep at home frozen. They keep for months if covered well and can be served with ice cream and coffee syrup for unexpected guests. Use the best white and dark chocolate you can get.

DARK CHOCOLATE BATTER

4 ounces unsweetened chocolate, chopped
6 tablespoons (3/4 stick) butter
2 eggs
1 egg yolk
1/2 teaspoon vanilla extract
1 1/2 cups sugar
1/2 cup all-purpose flour
2 tablespoons freeze-dried or granulated instant coffee
1/4 teaspoon salt

WHITE CHOCOLATE BATTER

5 ounces white chocolate
6 tablespoons (3/4 stick) butter
1 egg
1 egg white
1/2 teaspoon vanilla extract
1/4 teaspoon almond extract
1/2 cup sugar
1/2 cup all-purpose flour
1/4 teaspoon salt

1. Preheat the oven to 350°F. Butter and flour a 12 × 7 1/2 × 2-inch baking pan.

2. For the dark chocolate batter: place the unsweetened chocolate and butter together in a glass bowl and microwave on high for 45 seconds. Mix with a fork until evenly blended.

3. Mix the eggs, egg yolk, and vanilla extract in another small bowl.

4. Mix the sugar, flour, coffee, and salt in a large bowl with a fork. Pour in the chocolate and egg mixtures and mix with a fork or spatula until blended. Set aside.

5. For the white chocolate batter: place the white chocolate and butter in separate small glass bowls and microwave each on high for 30 seconds. Mix each with a fork until evenly melted.

6. Mix the egg, egg white, and extracts in another small bowl.

7. Mix the sugar, flour, and salt in a large bowl with a fork. Pour the white chocolate, butter, and egg mixture into the flour and mix with a fork or spatula until blended.

8. Pour both batters into the baking pan in dollops. Stir lightly with a fork or wooden skewer to blend and form swirls.

9. Bake for 45 minutes. Set aside to cool. Cut into squares and serve.

75

bars,
cookies,
and
goodies

coffee–almond clouds

Fill your mouth with this airy, delicious coffee and chocolate delicacy. Serve them with other filled tartlets for an assortment of sweets.

1 recipe almond pie dough (pg 25)
1 recipe caramel coffee sauce with amaretto (pg 33)
1 recipe coffee meringue frosting (pg 29)
Cocoa powder, optional
Powdered sugar, optional

Mini tartlet pans
Pastry bag with large, round 1A tip

1. Prepare the dough and allow it to rest in the refrigerator for 30 to 45 minutes. Preheat the oven to 375°F.

2. Roll the dough to 1/8-inch thickness, cut with a fluted cookie cutter, and set over each tartlet pan.

3. Place foil or paper cups over the dough, fill them with beans or weights, and bake 15 to 20 minutes, until golden. (You may keep the beans for future crusts.) Remove the foil or paper cups, and set the shells aside until they cool to room temperature.

4. Prepare the caramel coffee sauce and set aside to cool to room temperature.

5. Prepare the coffee meringue, and place into a pastry bag with a large, round 1A tip.

6. Spoon 1 teaspoon of the sauce into each tartlet shell, and then fill each tartlet with the meringue. When ready to serve, dust with cocoa powder or powdered sugar, if desired.

mocha delight
tartlets

Coffee and chocolate ... these
are mochaccinos in one bite!

1 recipe sweet pie dough (pg 26) with 2 tablespoons freeze-dried or
granulated instant coffee added
2/3 cup (1 recipe) dark chocolate ganache (pg 28)
1 cup (1/2 recipe) coffee pastry cream (pg 30)
2 ounces chocolate (dark, bittersweet, semisweet, or sweet), shaved (see tips,
pgs 38–39)

Mini tartlet pans

1. Prepare the dough, adding 2 tablespoons instant coffee with the flour,
    and allow to rest in the refrigerator for 30 to 45 minutes. Preheat the
    oven to 350°F.

2. Roll the dough to 1/8-inch thickness, cut with a fluted cookie cutter,
    and set over each tartlet pan.

3. Place foil or paper cups over the dough, fill them with beans or
    weights, and bake 15 to 20 minutes, until golden. (You may keep
    the beans for future crusts.) Remove the foil or paper cups, and set the
    shells aside until they cool to room temperature.

4. Prepare the ganache and pastry cream. Refrigerate until ready to use.

5. Spoon 1 1/2 teaspoons of ganache into each tartlet, and top with
    1 1/2 teaspoons of pastry cream. Decorate with chocolate shavings.

white chocolate

indulgence fruit tartlets

The freshness of fruit with the indulgence of white chocolate balance out guilt and pleasure.

1 recipe basic coffee pie dough (pg 25)
1 recipe white chocolate ganache (pg 28)
36 small whole strawberries, or 6 large strawberries hulled and sliced
5 to 6 kiwis, peeled and sliced
6 canned peach halves, drained thoroughly and sliced

1. Prepare the dough and allow it to rest in the refrigerator for 30 to 45 minutes. Preheat the oven to 375°F.

2. Roll the dough to 1/8-inch thickness, cut with a fluted cookie cutter, and set over each tartlet pan.

3. Place foil or paper cups over the dough, fill them with beans or weights, and bake 15 to 20 minutes, until golden. (You may keep the beans for future crusts.) Remove the foil or paper cups, and set the shells aside until they cool to room temperature.

4. Prepare the ganache and refrigerate until ready to use.

5. Spoon 1 1/2 teaspoons ganache into each tartlet shell. Decorate with strawberries, kiwis, and peaches.

white chocolate–
coffee
rum balls

Melt-in-your-mouth, truffle-like balls that can be served alone or used to decorate cakes. Handle them carefully, as they are delicate to the touch. If you want sturdier rum balls for traveling, you can add an extra half of a cake to the recipe.

1 11-ounce vanilla pound cake, cut into pieces (store-bought; thawed if frozen)
3 tablespoons dark rum
1 1/2 teaspoons freeze-dried or granulated instant coffee
3 ounces white chocolate, grated or chopped
1 cup chopped pecans, toasted
Unsweetened cocoa, powdered sugar, or ground almonds for coating*

1. Process the cake pieces to crumbs in a food processor, about 1 minute.

2. Mix the rum and coffee, pour over the cake, and process 10 seconds more. Add the pecans into the processor bowl.

3. Place the chocolate in a glass bowl and microwave on high for 20 seconds, mix with a fork, and add to the processor bowl. Process until a ball forms. Spread in a shallow pan or bowl, and refrigerate until set (overnight works best).

4. Scoop out 1-inch balls with a melon baller or small ice cream scoop, and place on a platter or baking sheet. They are very delicate, so return them to the refrigerator until hard again.

5. To coat the balls, place the cocoa, powdered sugar, or almonds in a plastic zipper bag. Add a few balls at a time and shake gently to coat completely.

6. Serve immediately, or refrigerate until ready to serve. The balls will hold their shape as long as they are not touched by warm hands.

*To coat 8 to 10 1-inch balls: 1 tablespoon cocoa, 2 tablespoons powdered sugar, or 2 tablespoons ground almonds

white chocolate–
coffee
truffles

Real white chocolate truffles—what a joy! As always, the best-quality chocolate will make these the star of the evening.

3 tablespoons sugar
1 tablespoon butter
1 tablespoon coffee liqueur
1 1/2 teaspoons freeze-dried or granulated instant coffee
3 ounces white chocolate, grated or chopped
Unsweetened cocoa, powdered sugar, or ground almonds for coating*

1. Place the chocolate in a medium bowl and set aside.

2. Place the sugar, butter, liqueur, and coffee in a nonstick sauté pan. Mix and cook over medium heat until all the sugar has dissolved, about 2 minutes.

3. Pour over the chocolate. Mix well with a fork until the chocolate melts. Refrigerate until set.

4. Scoop out 1/2-inch balls with a melon baller or small ice cream scoop, and place on a platter or baking sheet. They are very delicate, so return them to the refrigerator until hard again.

5. To coat the truffles, place the cocoa, powdered sugar, or almonds in a plastic zipper bag. Add a few truffles at a time and shake gently to coat completely.

6. Serve immediately, or refrigerate until ready to serve. The truffles will hold their shape as long as they are not touched by warm hands.

*To coat 16 to 20 1/2-inch truffles: 1 1/2 tablespoon cocoa, 3 tablespoons powdered sugar, or 3 tablespoons ground almonds

coconut coffee cocadas

This typical Columbian recipe usually is not prepared with coffee, but I have transformed it into a treat that is crunchy on the outside and chewy on the inside. You can keep them in tightly sealed containers or plastic zipper bags for 2 to 3 weeks.

2 coconuts, to yield 3 cups shredded fresh coconut and 1 cup coconut water
2 3/4 cups sugar
4 tablespoons freeze-dried or granulated instant coffee
1/4 cup water

1. Pick 1 or 2 large coconuts with plenty of water inside; this tells you they are fresh. Poke holes in the coconuts with an ice pick or clean screwdriver. Drain out the coconut water and set aside 1 cup. (Drink the rest—it is delicious and refreshing!)

2. Break open the coconuts with a hammer or mallet and remove the white meat with the tip of a sturdy knife. Peel off the brown skin from the coconut meat with a vegetable peeler or paring knife. Shred the white coconut meat to yield 3 cups.

3. Place sugar and coconut water into a heavy saucepan over medium heat, and stir to dissolve the sugar.

4. Add the shredded coconut. Decrease the heat to medium low and cook, stirring constantly, for 15 minutes.

5. Mix the coffee and water, add to the saucepan and cook for 5 to 7 minutes.

6. Spray a baking sheet with nonstick spray. Using 2 oiled forks, drop teaspoonful-sized scoops of the mixture onto the pan. Be careful, the mixture is hot.

7. Cool completely and enjoy!

83

bars,
cookies,
and
goodies

banana creamies

I love serving these party sweets on a 3-tiered serving platter. They are beautiful by themselves and displayed with other tartlets.

1 recipe almond pie dough (pg 25)
1 recipe bananas in coffee-caramel sauce (pg 32)
1 cup (1/2 recipe) coffee buttercream frosting (pg 29)
1/4 cup whole coffee beans

Mini tartlet pans
Pastry bag with a large star tube, 6B or 8B tip

1. Prepare the dough and allow it to rest in the refrigerator for 30 to 45 minutes. Preheat the oven to 375°F.

2. Roll the dough to 1/8-inch thickness, cut with a fluted cookie cutter, and set over each tartlet pan.

3. Place foil or paper cups over the dough, fill them with beans or weights, and bake 15 to 20 minutes, until golden. (You may keep the beans for future crusts.) Remove the foil or paper cups, and set the shells aside until they cool to room temperature.

4. Meanwhile, prepare the bananas in coffee-caramel sauce and set aside to cool.

5. Prepare the coffee buttercream frosting and place it in a pastry bag with a large star tube, 6B or 8B tip.

6. Place one banana slice with sauce in each tartlet shell. Top with a dollop of frosting, filling each tartlet. Decorate with coffee beans.

84

crunchy oatmeal

coffee cookies

Crunch is what makes these small sweet things stand out. They also travel and keep well so you can take them with you wherever you go and keep some stored at home for weeks … if they're not eaten before!

48 1-INCH COOKIES

1/2 pound clarified butter (see tips, pgs 38–39)
1 cup powdered sugar
1 teaspoon vanilla extract
2 tablespoons granulated instant coffee
1 cup all-purpose flour
1 cup raw oatmeal (rolled oats)
1 recipe caramel coffee sauce (pg 33)

1. Preheat the oven to 350°F. Line 3 baking sheets with waxed or parchment paper, and spray with nonstick spray.

2. Beat the butter and sugar in an electric mixer on medium speed for 6 to 8 minutes, or until light and fluffy. Mix in the vanilla extract.

3. In a small bowl, combine the coffee, flour, and oats. Add to the mixer bowl, reduce the speed to low, and beat only to incorporate, no more than 1 minute.

4. Form 1 tablespoon balls and place on the baking sheets. Bake for 10 to 12 minutes, until lightly golden. Remove from oven and set aside.

5. When the baking sheet is cool, peel the cookies off the paper and set on a rack. When they cool completely, store them in covered tins.

6. Drizzle with caramel coffee sauce when ready to serve.

85

bars,
cookies,
and
goodies

pecan coffee tart

Coffee adds a deep flavor to this rich dessert. The almond dough perfectly complements the pecan filling.

1 recipe almond pie dough (pg 25)
2 teaspoons freeze-dried or granulated instant coffee
1 teaspoon vanilla extract
2 eggs, lightly beaten
2/3 cup dark corn syrup
1/2 cup sugar
3 tablespoons concentrated coffee syrup (pgs 36–37)
1/4 teaspoon salt
1 cup pecan halves

10-inch tart pan

1. Prepare the pie dough and allow it to rest in the refrigerator for 30 to 45 minutes. Preheat the oven to 375°F.

2. In a small bowl, mix the coffee and vanilla extract.

3. In a medium bowl, blend the eggs, corn syrup, sugar, coffee syrup, and salt with a wire whisk. Add the coffee mixture and pecans.

4. Roll the dough to 1/8-inch thickness. Place into a 10-inch tart pan, and cut off the overhanging dough.

5. Pour the filling into the crust and spread the pecans evenly over the tart. (They will arrange themselves completely during baking). Bake for 35 to 45 minutes, until set in the center.

6. Remove from the oven and let cool for 15 to 30 minutes. Serve warm with ice cream or whipped cream.

the most moist cakes

The moist, buttery, and airy cakes in this chapter will make your mouth water. From the simple but scrumptious coconut-coffee cake to the light and chewy all-whites macadamia coffee cake, you will find a variety of textures and flavors to please any palate. The delicate coffee flavor in the cakes is sometimes complemented by elaborate frostings and other times by simple dustings of powdered sugar. Whatever your preference, there is something to please everyone in this chapter!

all-whites macadamia coffee cake

This is another recipe I decided to create after having so many leftover egg whites. It is soft and airy, and can be served with coffee or tea!

1 10-INCH TUBE CAKE OR 2 9-INCH LAYER CAKES

2 cups all-purpose flour
1 3/4 cups sugar (divided use)
1/4 cup ground macadamia nuts
1 tablespoon baking powder
4 tablespoons macadamia-flavored freeze-dried instant coffee
1/2 cup water
1/2 cup oil
1 1/2 teaspoons vanilla extract
5 egg whites
1/2 teaspoon cream of tartar
1/2 teaspoon salt

1. Preheat the oven to 350°F. Mix the flour, 1 cup of the sugar, nuts, baking powder, and coffee in the bowl of an electric mixer with a fork or whisk.

2. Make a well in the center and add the water, oil, and vanilla extract. Attach the mixer blades or paddle, and mix at medium-low speed for 2 to 3 minutes. Set aside.

3. In a clean mixer bowl, beat the egg whites, cream of tartar, and salt with clean beaters at medium-high speed until frothy, about 2 minutes. Slowly add the remaining 3/4 cup sugar, and mix on high speed for 8 minutes, until shiny and thick.

4. Fold the whites into the flour mixture. Pour into an ungreased 10-inch tube pan or 2 9-inch cake pans.

5. Bake for 45 to 50 minutes, until the cake springs back when touched and it feels sturdy.

6. Remove from the oven and cool in the pan upside down on a rack.

7. When completely cooled, pass a knife around the sides to loosen and remove the cake from the pan.

coffee
butter cake

A twist on traditional layer cakes, this basic cake recipe can be used with many fillings and frostings. It can also be baked in a loaf pan, cut into slices, and served as a snack.

1/2 pound (2 sticks) butter
1 1/2 cups sugar
3 eggs
1/2 teaspoon vanilla extract
3 cups all-purpose flour
4 tablespoons freeze-dried or granulated instant coffee
2 teaspoons baking powder
1/4 teaspoon baking soda
1/4 teaspoon salt
3/4 cup milk
1/4 cup sweet coffee syrup for drinks (pg 37)

1. Preheat the oven to 350°F. Butter and flour 2 8- or 9-inch cake pans.

2. Beat the butter and sugar in an electric mixer on low speed for 5 minutes, or until you have a creamy mixture.

3. Add the eggs one at a time until they are completely incorporated, about 2 minutes for each egg. Mix in the vanilla extract.

4. Mix the flour, coffee, baking powder, baking soda, and salt in a medium bowl with a fork. Add half of this mixture to the mixer bowl and mix for 30 seconds. Add half of the milk, and mix 30 seconds more. Repeat with the remaining flour mixture and milk. Mix in the coffee syrup.

5. Pour the batter into the cake pans. Bake for 45 to 50 minutes, until the cake springs back when touched and it feels sturdy.

6. Remove from the oven and cool in the pans on a rack, about 10 minutes. Remove from the pans and let cool completely.

91

the most
moist
cakes

coffee chiffon cake

Another cake that lends itself to many variations—serve it alone or with powdered sugar, fruit and cream, ice cream and caramel coffee sauce (pg 33), or even use it as the base of a very sophisticated dessert like the bombe café (pg 97). This is not a sweet cake; if serving it alone, reduce the coffee syrup to 3 tablespoons.

2 1/4 cups all-purpose flour
1 1/2 cups sugar (divided use)
1 tablespoon baking powder
5 eggs, separated
3/4 cup water
1/2 cup oil
4 tablespoons concentrated coffee syrup (pgs 36–37)
1 1/2 teaspoon vanilla extract
1/2 teaspoon almond extract
1/2 teaspoon cream of tartar
1/2 teaspoon salt

1. Preheat the oven to 350°F. Mix the flour, 1/2 cup of the sugar, and baking powder in the bowl of an electric mixer with a fork or whisk.

2. Make a well in the center and add the egg yolks, water, oil, coffee syrup, and extracts. Attach the mixer blades or paddle, and mix at medium-low speed for 2 to 3 minutes, until shiny. Set aside.

3. In a clean mixer bowl, beat the egg whites, cream of tartar, and salt with clean beaters at medium-high speed until frothy, about 2 minutes. Slowly add the remaining 1 cup sugar, and mix on high speed for 8 minutes, until shiny and thick.

4. Fold the whites into the flour mixture. Pour into an ungreased 10-inch tube or bowl pan, 2 9-inch cake pans, or 2 8-inch bowl pans.

5. Bake for 45 to 50 minutes, until the cake springs back when touched and it feels sturdy.

6. Remove from the oven and cool in the pan upside down on a rack.

7. When completely cooled, pass a knife around the sides to loosen and remove the cake from the pan.

VARIATION: For bowl cakes, line 2 8-inch or 1 10-inch stainless-steel or heatproof glass bowls with foil. Press the foil against the sides. (Cut enough foil so that it folds over the edges of the bowl.) Fill the 10-inch bowl with cake batter, or fill each 8-inch bowl with half of the batter. As soon as the cake comes out of the oven, set it upside down on a rack. Cool completely, remove the cake, and peel off the foil.

hot milk
cake

This highly absorbent cake is traditionally used for the *tres leches*, a milk-drenched cake that holds its shape and texture. You can also serve it with lemon or orange curd, passion fruit sauce (pgs 34–35), or coffee meringue frosting (pg 29)— or simply sprinkle with cinnamon and sugar before baking.

1 8 × 8-INCH CAKE

3 eggs
1 1/4 cup sugar
2 tablespoons butter
1/2 cup milk
2 tablespoons instant freeze-dried coffee
1 1/2 cups all-purpose flour
1/2 teaspoon baking powder
1/2 teaspoon baking soda
1/4 teaspoon salt
2 tablespoons concentrated coffee syrup (pg 36)
1/2 teaspoon vanilla extract

1. Preheat the oven to 350°F. Butter and flour an 8 × 8-inch pan.

2. Beat the eggs in an electric mixer at medium-high speed until frothy and pale, about 2 minutes. Add the sugar and beat for 6 to 8 minutes more, until shiny, thick, and almost white.

3. In a small saucepan, melt the butter in the milk. Stir in the coffee and set aside to cool to room temperature.

4. Combine the flour, baking powder, baking soda, and salt in a medium bowl with a fork. Add to the mixer bowl, reduce the speed to low, and mix for 30 seconds.

5. Add the milk and coffee mixture, coffee syrup, and vanilla extract to the mixer bowl. Mix only until incorporated, about 5 to 10 seconds.

6. Pour the batter into the pan. Bake for 30 to 40 minutes, until lightly golden.

7. Remove from the oven and cool in the pan on a rack. If you will be using this cake for either the three milks coffee delight (pg 106) or four milks coffee delight (pg 108), only allow to cool for 5 to 10 minutes.

hot milk

cake

This highly absorbent cake is traditionally used for the *tres leches*, a milk-drenched cake that holds its shape and texture. You can also serve it with lemon or orange curd, passion fruit sauce (pgs 34–35), or coffee meringue frosting (pg 29)— or simply sprinkle with cinnamon and sugar before baking.

1 8 × 8-INCH CAKE

3 eggs
1 1/4 cup sugar
2 tablespoons butter
1/2 cup milk
2 tablespoons instant freeze-dried coffee
1 1/2 cups all-purpose flour
1/2 teaspoon baking powder
1/2 teaspoon baking soda
1/4 teaspoon salt
2 tablespoons concentrated coffee syrup (pg 36)
1/2 teaspoon vanilla extract

1. Preheat the oven to 350°F. Butter and flour an 8 × 8-inch pan.

2. Beat the eggs in an electric mixer at medium-high speed until frothy and pale, about 2 minutes. Add the sugar and beat for 6 to 8 minutes more, until shiny, thick, and almost white.

3. In a small saucepan, melt the butter in the milk. Stir in the coffee and set aside to cool to room temperature.

4. Combine the flour, baking powder, baking soda, and salt in a medium bowl with a fork. Add to the mixer bowl, reduce the speed to low, and mix for 30 seconds.

5. Add the milk and coffee mixture, coffee syrup, and vanilla extract to the mixer bowl. Mix only until incorporated, about 5 to 10 seconds.

6. Pour the batter into the pan. Bake for 30 to 40 minutes, until lightly golden.

7. Remove from the oven and cool in the pan on a rack. If you will be using this cake for either the three milks coffee delight (pg 106) or four milks coffee delight (pg 108), only allow to cool for 5 to 10 minutes.

almond
coffee
meringue
cake

Ah, France! In the late 1970s and early 1980s, I learned how to make this meringue at the famous Lenôtre school in Paris. I have since taken this recipe and filled, frosted, and shaped the cakes in many different ways. Desserts like this take you back to a time when the best things came in small sizes.

2 10-INCH CAKES, 12 SERVINGS

4 10-inch (1 recipe) coffee meringue disks (pg 26)
1/4 cup (1/2 recipe) caramel coffee sauce (pg 33)
1 cup (1/2 recipe) coffee buttercream frosting (pg 29)
1 cup toasted sliced almonds (see tips, pg 38–39)
Powdered sugar and 12 almond slices for decoration

1. Prepare the meringue disks* and caramel sauce. Allow to cool. Prepare the buttercream frosting.

2. Place 2 meringue disks onto serving dishes. Spread each with half of the caramel sauce, top with a thin layer of frosting, and sprinkle each with 1/4 cup almonds. Cover each with another meringue disk.

3. Frost the sides of each layered cake, and then cover the frosted sides with the remaining almonds. Sprinkle with powdered sugar and decorate by forming a flower in the center with 6 almond slices.

4. Keep cakes at room temperature until ready to serve.

*If you have extra meringue, make more disks for another use.

almond liqueur bundt cake

CAKE

1/2 pound (2 sticks) butter
1 cup granulated sugar
3 eggs
1 teaspoon vanilla extract
2 tablespoons plus 4 teaspoons freeze-dried or granulated instant coffee (divided use)
2 1/2 cups all-purpose flour
1 1/2 teaspoons baking powder
1 teaspoon baking soda
1/4 teaspoon salt
1/2 cup plain yogurt
2 1/2 tablespoons amaretto
1/2 cup light brown sugar
1/2 cup toasted slivered almonds (see tips, pgs 38–39)

This super-moist Bundt cake is small and full of flavor. A great cake for tea time, or after a meal. It also travels very well.

GLAZE

1/4 cup water
3 tablespoons sugar
1/4 cup amaretto
2 tablespoons freeze-dried or powdered instant coffee

8- or 9-inch Bundt pan

1. Preheat the oven to 350°F. Butter and lightly flour a Bundt pan.

2. Beat the butter and granulated sugar in an electric mixer at low speed for 5 minutes, or until you have a creamy mixture.

3. Add the eggs one at a time until they are completely incorporated, about 2 minutes for each egg. Mix the vanilla and 2 teaspoons of the coffee, and add to the mixer bowl.

4. Combine the flour, baking powder, baking soda, salt, and 2 tablespoons of the coffee in a medium bowl with a fork. Add half to the mixer bowl and mix for 30 seconds. Add the yogurt and mix for 30 seconds more. Add the rest of the flour mixture and mix only until incorporated.

5. In a small bowl, dissolve the remaining 2 teaspoons of coffee in the amaretto. Mix in the brown sugar and almonds and set aside.

6. Pour 3/4 of the batter into the pan. Top with the almond-amaretto mixture, and then add remaining batter. Slightly mix them with a wooden skewer.

7. Bake for 1 hour, or until the cake springs back when touched and it feels sturdy. Remove from oven, set aside to cool on a rack for 15 to 20 minutes, and remove the cake from the pan.

8. While the cake is cooling, make the glaze. Bring the sugar and water to a boil in a small saucepan over low heat, until dissolved. Remove from heat and add the amaretto and coffee. Immediately brush the cake with the glaze, and cool completely before serving.

bombe
café

This is a simple, yet very impressive, version of a white chocolate bombe I once created with a leftover chiffon dome cake. Great as a dessert or as a gift to a very important person!

1 8-inch bowl (1/2 recipe) coffee chiffon cake (pg 92)
1/2 cup (1/4 recipe) coffee pastry cream (pg 30)
3 tablespoons heavy cream
2/3 cup (1 recipe) dark chocolate ganache (pg 28)
1/4 cup sugar
4 tablespoons water (divided use)
1 1/2 teaspoons freeze-dried or granulated instant coffee
1 1/2 tablespoons coffee liqueur
1/2 cup toasted almonds, ground (see tips, pgs 38–39)

1. The day before you assemble the bombe, prepare the chiffon cake and the pastry cream. Cover the pastry cream with plastic or waxed paper, and refrigerate to set. (To hasten setting, refrigerate the cream in a shallow dish.)

2. Mix the heavy cream into the cold pastry cream with a wire whisk or spatula. Prepare the ganache and refrigerate until cool and thick enough to cover the dessert.

3. When you're ready to assemble the dessert, make a syrup by bringing the sugar and 3 tablespoons of the water to a boil in a small saucepan. Reduce the heat to medium, and simmer for 3 minutes. Remove from the heat. Mix the remaining tablespoon of water with the coffee and add to the saucepan. Stir in the liqueur, and set aside to cool.

4. Turn the cake upside down and remove from the pan onto a serving plate. Slice the cake horizontally into 4 layers.

5. Remove the top 3 layers and brush the bottom one with the syrup, spread with 3 tablespoons of the pastry cream, and sprinkle with about 1/4 of the almonds. Cover with next layer and repeat until topping with the final layer.

6. Frost the cake with the ganache and sprinkle with the remaining almonds.

7. Refrigerate overnight or quickly cool in the freezer for 30 minutes.

97

the most
moist
cakes

caramel
pecan cake

One bite of this buttery pecan delight
is worth all of the effort to make it.
It also makes a great birthday cake.

1 10-inch tube (1 recipe) coffee chiffon cake (pg 92)
1 cup (1/2 recipe) cream cheese–coffee buttercream frosting (pg 30)
2 cups (1 recipe) coffee buttercream frosting (pg 29)
2 cups (1 recipe) caramelized coffee pecans (pg 28)

1. Prepare the coffee chiffon cake. Cool and slice it horizontally into 4
    layers. Prepare the buttercream frostings. Prepare the caramelized
    coffee pecans, reserve 8 pecan halves, and chop the rest.

2. Place the bottom cake layer on a serving dish. Spread with half of
    the cream cheese–coffee buttercream frosting. (It will be a thin layer.)
    Sprinkle with 1/4 of the chopped pecans.

3. Place the next cake layer over this and spread with 1/4 of the
    coffee buttercream frosting. Sprinkle with 1/4 of the chopped pecans

4. Place the next cake layer over this and spread with the remaining half
    of the cream cheese–coffee buttercream frosting. Sprinkle with 1/4 of
    the chopped pecans.

5. Cover with the top cake layer. Frost the entire cake with the remaining
    coffee buttercream frosting. Cover the sides with the remaining chopped
    pecans, and decorate the top with the reserved pecan halves.

cherry-coffee
chiffon cake

This large grandma-style cake
will be a hit at any family event!

2 9-inch (1 recipe) vanilla-and-coffee-dotted chiffon cakes (pg 112)*
2 cups (1 recipe) coffee buttercream frosting (pg 29)
1/2 cup basic simple syrup (pg 36)
1 cup (1 recipe) white chocolate coffee sauce (pg 35)
1 10-ounce jar maraschino cherries in syrup
2 tablespoons vodka
1 tablespoon freeze-dried or granulated instant coffee
Whole coffee beans

1. Prepare the chiffon cake, frosting, simple syrup, and white chocolate coffee sauce and let them cool completely.

2. Drain the jar of cherries. Reserve 8 whole cherries for decoration, cut the remaining cherries into quarters, and set aside.

3. Mix the vodka and coffee in a small bowl, until the coffee is dissolved. Stir in the simple syrup.

4. Cut each 9-inch layer cake horizontally. (If using a 10-inch tube cake, cut it horizontally into 4 layers.)

5. Place the bottom cake layer on a serving dish. Brush with coffee-syrup. Spread with 2 to 3 tablespoons of chocolate sauce, and cover with 1/3 of the chopped cherries. Repeat with two more cake layers.

6. Place the final cake layer on top. Frost the entire cake and decorate the top with the reserved whole cherries and coffee beans.

7. Refrigerate overnight or quickly cool in the freezer for 30 minutes.

*You may also use a 10-inch tube cake.

99

the most
moist
cakes

chocolate-
spiced
chiffon cake

This is often a base for other cakes and desserts, but it can also be served on its own with caramel coffee sauce (pg 33) and powdered sugar. It's perfect for a summer picnic.

1 10-INCH TUBE CAKE OR 2 8-INCH BOWL CAKES

1 3/4 cups plus 2 tablespoons all-purpose flour
2 cups sugar (divided use)
1/2 cup unsweetened cocoa
2 tablespoons freeze-dried or powdered instant coffee
1 tablespoon baking powder
1/2 teaspoon ground cinnamon
1/2 teaspoon chili powder
5 eggs, separated
3/4 cup water
1/2 cup oil
1 1/2 teaspoons vanilla extract
1/2 teaspoon cream of tartar
1/2 teaspoon salt

1. Preheat the oven to 350°F. (For bowl cakes, see variation, pg 92)

2. Mix the flour, 1 cup of the sugar, cocoa, coffee, baking powder, cinnamon, and chili powder in the bowl of an electric mixer with a fork. Make a well in the center and add the egg yolks, water, oil, and vanilla extract. Attach the mixer blades or paddle, and mix at medium-low speed for 2 to 3 minutes, until shiny.

3. In a clean mixer bowl, beat the egg whites, cream of tartar, and salt with clean beaters at medium-high speed until frothy, about 2 minutes. Slowly add the remaining 1 cup of sugar, and mix at high speed for 8 minutes, until shiny and thick. Fold the whites into the flour mixture.

4. Pour the batter into an ungreased tube pan or the prepared bowls. Bake for 45 to 50 minutes, until the cake springs back when touched and it feels sturdy.

5. Remove from the oven and cool in the pan upside down on a rack.

6. When completely cooled, pass a knife around the sides to loosen and remove the cake from the pan.

chocolate chip and coffee chiffon cake

This cake is also often a base for many desserts, but it is a beauty and can stand on its own! A glass of ice wine or pink champagne will take it to the next level!

1 10-INCH TUBE CAKE, 2 9-INCH CAKE LAYERS, 2 8-INCH BOWL CAKES, OR 1 10-INCH BOWL CAKE

2 1/4 cups all-purpose flour
1 1/2 cups sugar (divided use)
1 tablespoon baking powder
5 eggs, separated
3/4 cup water
1/2 cup oil
4 tablespoons concentrated coffee syrup (pgs 36–37)
1 1/2 teaspoons vanilla extract
1/2 teaspoon cream of tartar
1/2 teaspoon salt
1/2 cup milk chocolate chips

1. Preheat the oven to 350°F. (For bowl cakes, see variation, pg 92)

2. Mix the flour, 1/2 cup of the sugar, and baking powder in the bowl of an electric mixer with a fork. Make a well in the center and add the egg yolks, water, oil, coffee syrup, and vanilla extract. Attach the mixer blades or paddle, and mix at medium-low speed for 2 to 3 minutes, until shiny.

3. In a clean mixer bowl, beat the egg whites, cream of tartar, and salt with clean beaters at medium-high speed until frothy, about 2 minutes. Slowly add the remaining 1 cup of sugar, and mix at high speed for 8 minutes, until shiny and thick. Fold the whites into the flour mixture, and then fold in the chocolate chips.

4. Pour the batter into an ungreased tube pan or the prepared bowls. Bake for 45 to 50 minutes, until the cake springs back when touched and it feels sturdy.

5. Remove from the oven and cool in the pan upside down on a rack.

6. When completely cooled, pass a knife around the sides to loosen and remove the cake from the pan.

the most
moist
cakes

coconut coffee cake

2 1/4 cups all-purpose flour
1 cup granulated sugar
1 cup dark brown sugar
1 cup toasted almonds, chopped (see tips, pgs 38–39)
3/4 teaspoons baking powder
3/4 teaspoon baking soda
1/4 teaspoon salt
3 eggs
1 cup sweetened coconut flakes (divided use)
3/4 cup coconut milk
1/2 cup oil
1/4 cup concentrated coffee syrup (pgs 36–37)
1/2 teaspoon vanilla extract
1/4 teaspoon almond extract
1 cup (1 recipe) espresso buttercream frosting (pg 31)

Imagine being in the sunny Caribbean with all of the palm trees, the ocean, and this wonderfully delicious cake. It takes only minutes to prepare—and the oven does the rest.

8- or 9-inch Bundt pan

1. Preheat the oven to 350°F. Butter and lightly flour a Bundt pan.

2. Mix the flour, sugars, almonds, baking powder, baking soda, and salt in the bowl of an electric mixer with a fork. Make a well in the center and add the eggs, 3/4 cup of the coconut flakes, coconut milk, oil, coffee syrup, and extracts. Attach the mixer blades or paddle, and mix at medium-low speed for 1 minute.

3. Pour the batter into the prepared Bundt pan. Bake for 45 to 55 minutes, until the cake springs back when touched and it feels sturdy.

4. Remove from the oven and cool in the pan for 15 to 20 minutes, then remove from the pan and let cool completely.

5. Frost and sprinkle with leftover coconut flakes.

coffee-
almond
caramel
roll

Fit for royalty! Along with the bombes, this cake reaches the height of taste and elegance. It can be prepared ahead of time and frozen before adding the outer praline. Take care to wrap it very well so that the delicate ingredients are not altered in the freezer.

1 15-INCH JELLY ROLL, 16 SERVINGS

1 1/2 cups (1 recipe) coffee crème charlotte (pg 140)
1 recipe almond caramel praline (pg 27)
1 recipe coffee jelly roll (pg 115)

WHIPPED CREAM
1 cup heavy cream
1/2 cup powdered sugar
1 tablespoon cognac
1 1/2 teaspoons concentrated coffee syrup (pgs 36–37)

1. Prepare the coffee crème charlotte up to 1 day ahead. Prepare the praline, chop half into small bits and half into 1-inch pieces, and store in plastic zipper bags.

2. Prepare the jelly roll and roll onto plastic wrap or a clean cloth.

3. Spread the thickened coffee crème charlotte over the roll, sprinkle with the praline bits, and roll up lengthwise. Wrap the roll tightly with plastic wrap and refrigerate to set, about 30 minutes.

4. To prepare the whipped cream, beat the cream and sugar in a clean, dry mixer bowl at high speed for 1 1/2 to 2 minutes or until soft peaks form. Add the cognac and syrup, and beat to stiff peaks.

5. When ready to frost, remove the wrap and place the roll on a serving dish. Frost with a light coat of whipped cream and cover with the large praline pieces.

coffee

chocolate
chip cake

This cake brings out the kid in me.
I love chocolate chips!

12 TO 16 SERVINGS

CAKE
1/2 pound (2 sticks) butter
1 1/4 cups granulated sugar
3/4 cup chocolate chips
3 eggs
1 teaspoon vanilla extract
2 1/2 cups all-purpose flour
2 1/2 tablespoons freeze-dried or granulated instant coffee
1 1/2 teaspoons baking powder
1/2 teaspoon baking soda
1/4 teaspoon salt
3/4 cup plain yogurt or buttermilk

ICING
1 cup powdered sugar
2 1/2 tablespoons heavy cream
2 teaspoons freeze-dried or granulated instant coffee
1 1/2 teaspoons añejo rum*

1 8-inch Bundt pan

1. Preheat the oven to 350°F. Butter and lightly flour a Bundt pan.

2. Beat the butter and granulated sugar in an electric mixer at low speed for 5 minutes, or until you have a creamy mixture. Add the chocolate chips and mix for 1 minute more.

3. Add the eggs one at a time, and mix at low speed until they are completely incorporated, about 2 minutes for each egg. Add the vanilla extract and mix for 10 seconds more.

4. Mix the flour, coffee, baking powder, baking soda, and salt in a medium bowl with a fork. Add 1/3 to the mixer bowl and mix for 30 seconds, then add half the yogurt or buttermilk and mix for 30 seconds. Repeat until all of the flour mixture and yogurt are added.

5. Pour the batter into the prepared Bundt pan. Bake for 45 to 55 minutes, until the cake springs back when touched and it feels sturdy.

6. Remove from the oven and cool in the pan for 15 to 20 minutes, then remove from the pan and let cool completely.

7. To make the icing, mix the powdered sugar, cream, coffee, and rum in an electric mixer for 30 to 45 seconds, until smooth. Pour over the completely cooled cake in swirls. Let set for 5 minutes and then serve.

*Añejo rum is a golden blend of rich, aged rums with a mellow taste and rich aroma.

dulce
de leche
cake

The sweet *dulce de leche* and the vodka syrup contrast nicely in this cake. Try the coffee-infused *dulce de leche* on its own, or add a dollop of it to coffee ice cream.

2 8-inch layer (1 recipe) coffee butter cakes (pg 91)
3 cups (1 recipe) coffee meringue frosting (pg 29)
1/2 cup sugar
1/3 cup water
1 1/2 tablespoons vodka
1/2 cup *dulce de leche* (pg 24)
2 1/2 teaspoons concentrated coffee syrup (pgs 36–37)

1. Prepare the coffee butter cakes, cool, and slice each in half horizontally. Prepare the frosting.

2. Combine the sugar and water in a small saucepan. Bring to a boil and remove from the heat. Stir in the vodka.

3. Mix the *dulce de leche* and coffee syrup in a small bowl.

4. Place a bottom cake layer on a serving dish, and brush with the vodka syrup. Spread with half of the *dulce de leche* mixture. (It will be a thin layer.)

5. Place the next half layer on top. Brush with the vodka syrup and spread with 1 cup of the meringue frosting.

6. Place the next half layer on top. Brush with the vodka syrup and spread the remaining *dulce de leche* mixture.

7. Cover with the last half layer and brush with any remaining vodka syrup. Frost the whole cake with the remaining meringue frosting.

105

the most
moist
cakes

three
milks
coffee
delight

Tres Leches (Three Milks), and the
recently developed *Cuatro Leches*
(Four Milks) are traditional Latin
American desserts. I have modified
them to include a touch of coffee.

1 recipe hot milk cake (pg 94)

THREE MILKS SAUCE
1 1/2 cups evaporated milk
1 1/2 cups condensed milk
3/4 cup heavy cream
4 1/2 tablespoons freeze-dried or granulated instant coffee

1/2 cup (1 recipe) concentrated coffee syrup (pgs 36–37)

1. Prepare the hot milk cake. Remove the cake from the oven and allow to cool in the baking pan for 5 to 10 minutes.

2. Combine the evaporated milk, condensed milk, cream, and coffee in a medium saucepan. Stir continuously over medium heat until it comes to a simmer. Remove from the heat, set aside.

3. Prick the cake with a fork and pour the three milks sauce over it. Let the sauce absorb.

4. Cut the desert into rounds with 1 1/2- or 2-inch cookie cutters and place on individual serving plates. Pour some of the remaining three milks sauce over each piece, and drizzle with the concentrated coffee syrup.

VARIATIONS: Frost with 1 1/2 cups (1/2 recipe) coffee meringue frosting (pg 29) and serve with a coffee sauce on the side. You can also fill the cake with 1 cup of coffee pastry cream (pg 30). While the cake is still warm, remove it from the pan and split it horizontally into 2 layers. Spread the bottom layer with the pastry cream, return it to the pan, replace the top layer, and proceed to steps 3 and 4.

four milks
coffee
delight

Talk about overindulgence!
This dessert is divine.

8 TO 10 SERVINGS

1 recipe hot milk cake (pg 94)

FOUR MILKS SAUCE
1 cup evaporated milk
1 cup condensed milk
1/2 cup heavy cream
3 tablespoons freeze-dried or granulated instant coffee

1/2 cup *dulce de leche* (pg 24)
3 tablespoons concentrated coffee syrup (pgs 36–37)
1 recipe almond caramel praline (pg 27)
1 cup (1 recipe) white chocolate coffee sauce (pg 35)

1. Prepare the hot milk cake. Remove the cake from the oven and allow to cool in the baking pan for 5 to 10 minutes.

2. Combine the evaporated milk, condensed milk, cream, and coffee in a medium saucepan. Stir continuously over medium heat until it comes to a simmer. Remove from the heat, set aside.

3. Mix the *dulce de leche* and coffee syrup in a separate bowl, set aside. Slice the cake horizontally into thirds, and return the slices to the pan spreading the *dulce de leche* mixture onto the two bottom slices.

4. Prick the cake with a fork and pour the four milks sauce over it. Continue adding sauce until half of it is absorbed. Refrigerate the cake until completely cool.

5. Prepare the praline and break into 1- to 2-inch chunks. Prepare the white chocolate sauce and set aside until ready to serve.

6. Cut the desert into rounds with 1 1/2- or 2-inch cookie cutters and place on individual serving plates. Pour the white chocolate sauce over each piece and decorate with a piece of praline.

7. Refrigerate and serve cold.

starburst
cake

Imagine eating a chocolate bar
as light as a cloud. This is it!

16 SERVINGS

2 8-inch layer (1 recipe) coffee butter cake (pg 89)
2/3 cup (1 recipe) dark chocolate ganache (pg 28)
1/2 cup (1 recipe) caramel coffee sauce (pg 33)
2 cups (1 recipe) cream cheese–coffee buttercream frosting (pg 30)
1/2 cup roasted unsalted peanuts, optional

1. Prepare the coffee butter cakes. Cut each cake in half horizontally. Prepare the chocolate ganache, set aside 2 tablespoons. Prepare the caramel coffee sauce and cool to room temperature. Prepare the cream cheese–coffee buttercream frosting.

2. Place one cake half layer on a serving dish. Spread with 1/3 of the chocolate ganache in a thin layer, top with 1/3 of the caramel sauce, and sprinkle 1/3 of the peanuts. Repeat with two more layers, and place the last half layer of cake on top.

3. Frost entire cake with the buttercream frosting.

4. Using a pastry bag or plastic bag (see tips, 38–39), decorate the top with chocolate dots to form a star.

5. Keep at room temperature and serve.

the most
moist
cakes

strawberry
coffee
surprise

The surprise in this airy yet rich
desert is fresh, sweet strawberries
hidden between the creamy
frosting and cake layers. They
add a wonderful burst of flavor.

2 9-inch layer (1 recipe) coffee chiffon cakes (pg 92)
2 cups (1 recipe) cream cheese—coffee buttercream frosting (pg 30)
2 pints strawberries
1/2 cup sugar
1/3 cup water (divided use)
2 teaspoons freeze-dried or granulated instant coffee
1 1/2 tablespoons tequila

1. Prepare the coffee chiffon cake layers. Cool and cut each cake in half horizontally. Prepare the frosting and refrigerate until ready to use.

2. Set aside 6 to 8 of the best-looking strawberries and slice the rest.

3. Bring the sugar and 1/4 cup water to a boil in a small saucepan, reduce the heat to medium, simmer for 3 minutes, then remove from heat. Mix the remaining water with the coffee, and add to the saucepan. Stir in the tequila. Set aside to cool.

4. Place the bottom half layer on a serving dish, and brush with the syrup. Spread with a thin layer of frosting (about 1/3 cup), and cover with 1/3 of the sliced strawberries. Repeat with two more layers, and place the last half layer of cake on top.

5. Frost the entire cake with the remaining buttercream, and decorate the top with the reserved whole strawberries.

queen's

celebration
roll

1 recipe coffee jelly roll (pg 115)
2/3 cup (1 recipe) dark chocolate ganache (pg 28)
1 cup (1 recipe) espresso buttercream frosting (pg 31)
1 cup (1/2 recipe) caramelized coffee pecans (pg 28)

1. Prepare the jelly roll, ganache, frosting, and pecans. Set aside 8 pecans and grind the rest in a food processor for 7 seconds, about 3 pulses.

2. Unroll the jelly roll and lay flat over plastic wrap or parchment.

3. Spread all of the ganache over the roll. Roll it up tightly and place seam side down on a rectangular serving dish.

4. Frost the entire roll, and cover the sides with the chopped pecans. Decorate the top with the pecan halves and serve.

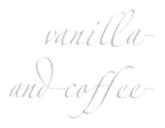

dotted chiffon cake

2 1/4 cups all-purpose flour
1 1/2 cups sugar (divided use)
1 tablespoon baking powder
5 eggs, separated
3/4 cup water
1/2 cup oil
1 1/2 teaspoons vanilla extract
1/2 teaspoon almond extract
1/2 teaspoon cream of tartar
1/2 teaspoon salt
2 tablespoons freeze-dried or granulated instant coffee

1. Preheat the oven to 350°F. (For bowl cakes, see variation, pg 92)

2. Mix the flour, 1 cup of the sugar, and baking powder in the bowl of an electric mixer with a fork. Make a well in the center and add the egg yolks, water, oil, and extracts. Attach the mixer blades or paddle, and mix at medium-low speed for 2 to 3 minutes, until shiny.

3. In a clean mixer bowl, beat the egg whites, cream of tartar, and salt with clean beaters at medium-high speed until frothy, about 2 minutes. Slowly add the remaining 1/2 cup sugar, and mix at high speed for 8 minutes, until shiny and thick.

4. Fold the whites into the flour mixture. Fold in the coffee. Pour into an ungreased pan.

5. Bake for 45 to 50 minutes, until the cake springs back when touched and it feels sturdy.

6. Remove from the oven and cool in the pan upside down on a rack.

7. When completely cooled, pass a knife around the sides to loosen and remove the cake from the pan.

white chocolate–

coffee surprise

The "surprise" can be a wrapped note, a ring, or even a copy of a flight reservation—what a tasty way to give someone a gift!

1 10-inch tube (1 recipe) chocolate chip and coffee chiffon cake (pg 101)
2/3 cup (1 recipe) white chocolate ganache (pg 28)
3 cups (1 recipe) coffee meringue frosting (pg 29)
1/2 cup sugar
1/3 cup water (divided use)
2 teaspoons freeze-dried or granulated instant coffee
1 1/2 tablespoons cognac or vodka
A surprise gift

Kitchen torch, optional

1. Prepare the chiffon cake. Cool and slice into 4 layers. Prepare the ganache, cool, and place in the freezer for 15 minutes, or until it thickens. Prepare the frosting.

2. Bring the sugar and 1/4 cup water to a boil in a small saucepan, reduce heat to medium, simmer for 3 minutes, then remove from heat. Mix the remaining water with the coffee in a small bowl, and add to the saucepan. Stir in the cognac, and let cool.

3. Place the bottom cake layer on a serving dish. Brush with the syrup, and spread with half of the ganache. (It will be a thin layer.)

4. Top with another layer of cake, brush with syrup, and spread with frosting. Add the next layer, brush with syrup, and spread with the remaining ganache. Cover with the last cake layer.

5. Place a small wrapped surprise in the tubular center of the cake.

6. Frost the entire cake with the remaining frosting. If you have a small kitchen torch, you can caramelize the outside.

mocha

cake

A cake with a subtle coffee flavor and a frosting that just melts in your mouth. The rum syrup adds a festive touch, but can be omitted if desired.

2 8-inch layer (1 recipe) coffee butter cakes (pg 91)
3 cups (1 recipe) coffee meringue frosting (pg 29)
2/3 cup (1 recipe) dark or white chocolate ganache (pg 28),
   plus extra for decorating, optional
1/2 cup sugar
1/3 cup water
1 1/2 tablespoons light rum

1. Prepare the coffee butter cakes. Cool and slice each cake in half horizontally. Prepare the frosting and ganache.

2. Combine the sugar and water in a small saucepan. Bring to a boil and remove from heat. Stir in the rum.

3. Place a half layer of cake on a serving dish. Brush with the rum syrup and spread with half of the ganache. (It will be a thin layer.)

4. Top with the next half layer. Brush with syrup and cover with half of the meringue frosting. Add the next layer, brush with syrup, and spread with the remaining ganache. Cover with the last half layer.

5. Brush with any remaining rum syrup and frost the entire cake with the remaining meringue frosting.

6. If desired, decorate with extra ganache using a pastry bag or plastic bag (see tips, pgs 38–39).

coffee
jelly roll

1 cup all-purpose flour
1 cup granulated sugar (divided use)
2 teaspoons baking powder*
3 eggs, separated
1/2 cup water
1/3 cup oil
3 tablespoons concentrated coffee syrup (pg 36–37) or espresso
1 teaspoon vanilla extract
1/4 teaspoon cream of tartar
1/4 teaspoon salt
Powdered sugar

Jelly rolls are very versatile—you can roll, cut, stack, fill, and frost them in many different ways. They are great decorated with fresh fruit, almond pralines, or chocolate ganache.

1. Preheat the oven to 425°F. Butter a 10 1/2 × 15 1/2-inch jelly roll pan and line it with waxed or parchment paper.

2. Mix the flour, 1/2 cup sugar, and baking powder in the bowl of an electric mixer with a fork. Make a well in the center and add the egg yolks, water, oil, coffee syrup, and vanilla extract. Attach the mixer blades or paddle, and mix at medium-low speed for 2 to 3 minutes, until thoroughly mixed.

3. In a clean mixer bowl, beat the egg whites, cream of tartar, and salt with clean beaters at medium-high speed until frothy, about 2 minutes. Slowly add the remaining 1/2 cup of sugar, and mix at high speed for 3 minutes, until shiny and thick.

4. Reduce speed to low and slowly pour the flour mixture into the whites, just to combine. Turn off the mixer, scrape the bowl, and mix further with a spatula.

5. Pour the batter into the jelly roll pan. Bake for 12 to 15 minutes, until lightly golden.

6. Remove from the oven and turn upside down onto a cloth or waxed paper covered with powdered sugar. Lift the pan, peel away the paper, and cover with a clean towel.

*For a 1/4-inch-thick jelly roll, omit the baking powder.

VARIATIONS: For a mocha jelly roll, add 1 1/2 teaspoons of cocoa to the flour mixture in step 3. For a chocolate jelly roll, omit the instant coffee, and add 2 tablespoons of cocoa to the flour mixture in step 3.

rum cake
"mamina"

My mother's rum cake oozes with a nutty, rich filling. It's great with tea!

1 8-INCH TUBE PAN

CAKE

8 tablespoons (1 stick) butter
1 1/4 cups granulated sugar
2 eggs
2 tablespoons powdered or granulated instant coffee (divided use)
1 tablespoon dark rum
1/2 teaspoon vanilla extract
2 cups all-purpose flour
3/4 teaspoon baking powder
3/4 teaspoon baking soda
1/4 teaspoon salt
1 1/4 cups buttermilk
1/2 cup dried cranberries
1/2 cup chopped walnuts
1/4 cup light brown sugar
1 teaspoon ground cinnamon

GLAZE

1 cup powdered sugar
3 tablespoons brewed espresso or 1 tablespoon concentrated coffee syrup (pgs 36–37)
1/2 teaspoon heavy cream (increase to 2 tablespoons if using coffee syrup)
1/4 teaspoon vanilla extract

1. Preheat the oven to 350°F. Butter and flour a 8-inch tube pan.

2. Beat the butter and granulated sugar in an electric mixer at low speed for 5 minutes, or until you have a creamy mixture. Add the eggs one at a time until they are completely incorporated, about 2 minutes for each egg.

3. Mix 1 tablespoon of the coffee, rum, and vanilla extract in a small bowl. Add to the mixer bowl and mix for 1 minute.

4. In a medium bowl, mix the flour, baking powder, baking soda, and salt with a fork. Add half of this mixture to the mixer bowl and mix for 30 seconds. Add half of the buttermilk and mix for 30 seconds more. Add the remaining flour and buttermilk, and mix just until blended.

5. In a small bowl, mix cranberries, walnuts, brown sugar, remaining 1 tablespoon coffee, and cinnamon. Pour half of the batter into the pan and sprinkle 3/4 of the cranberry-nut mixture, making sure it does not reach the sides or it will caramelize and stick to the pan. Pour the rest of the batter over the nuts, and sprinkle the remaining nut mixture on top.

6. Bake for 45 to 50 minutes, until the cake springs back when touched and it feels sturdy. Remove from oven and cool in the pan on a rack for about 10 minutes. Remove from pan, and cool completely.

7. While the cake is cooling, mix the powdered sugar, espresso or coffee syrup, cream, and vanilla extract. Drizzle over the cake and serve.

the most
moist
cakes

cool desserts

Indulge yourself in these creamy coffee concoctions that are designed to delight all of your senses. The white chocolate mousses and glossy bombes are cool in temperature, as well as flavor and style. The cheesecakes are flavored with aromatic rum, crunchy toasted almonds, smooth coffee caramel, and chunky chocolate chips. Eat the rich ice creams on their own, or use them to prepare the fabulous shakes and bomba cups.

cooked coffee

ice cream

1 cup heavy cream
2 cups 2% milk
2/3 cup granulated sugar
1/4 cup brown sugar
3 egg yolks
4 tablespoons freeze-dried or granulated instant coffee
1/8 teaspoon salt
1 teaspoon vanilla extract

Ice cream maker

1. Beat the cream, milk, sugars, egg yolks, coffee, and salt in a large bowl.

2. Transfer to a heavy saucepan and cook over medium heat, stirring constantly, until the brown sugar has dissolved and the mixture has thickened, about 7 to 8 minutes. Remove from heat and stir in the vanilla extract.

3. Strain into a bowl and refrigerate until completely cold.

4. Transfer to ice cream maker and process until thick and creamy.

5. Freeze to desired hardness and serve. For best consistency, freeze overnight.

VARIATION: For mocha ice cream, melt 3 ounces of sweet chocolate in the microwave and add it to the mixture along with the vanilla extract. Mix with a wire whisk and continue with step 2.

120

coffee praline

ice cream (uncooked)

1 1/2 cups heavy cream
2 cups 2% milk
2/3 cup granulated sugar
1/4 cup brown sugar
4 tablespoons freeze-dried or granulated instant coffee
1/8 teaspoon salt
3/4 cup (about 1/2 recipe) ground almond caramel praline (pg 27)

Ice cream machine

1. Beat the cream, milk, sugars, coffee, and salt in a large bowl.

2. Transfer to a blender, mix, and refrigerate until cold.

3. Transfer to ice cream maker and process until thick and creamy. Mix in the praline.

4. Freeze to desired hardness and serve. For best consistency, freeze overnight.

121

coffee macadamia
ice cream
(cooked)

3/4 cup sugar
3/4 cup water
1 1/2 cups evaporated milk
1 1/2 cups heavy cream
3 egg yolks
1/8 teaspoon salt
4 1/2 tablespoons macadamia-flavored freeze-dried instant coffee
1 teaspoon vanilla extract
1 cup chocolate-covered macadamias, chopped

Ice cream maker

1. Bring the sugar and water to a boil in a small saucepan, cook until sugar is dissolved. Remove from heat and let syrup cool to room temperature.

2. In a blender, combine the syrup, milk, cream, egg yolks, and salt. Transfer to a heavy saucepan and cook over medium heat, stirring constantly, until the mixture has thickened, about 7 minutes.

3. Remove from the heat and stir in the coffee and vanilla extract. Refrigerate until completely cold.

4. Transfer to ice cream maker and process until thick and creamy. Mix in the chopped macadamias.

5. Freeze to desired hardness and serve. For best consistency, freeze overnight.

bomba

This dessert was created during a party at my house honoring three Japanese chefs. I forgot to prepare dessert, but because I was in the middle of creating the recipes for this book I had lots of coffee products in my freezer and fridge. When I served the dessert to one of the Japanese chefs who spoke no English or Spanish, he just said "Café Bomba."

12 SERVINGS

1/2 cup sweet coffee syrup (pg 37)
About 1 pint (1 recipe) cooked coffee ice cream (pg 120)
3/4 cup (1/2 recipe) coffee crème anglaise sauce (pg 33)
3/4 cup vodka

12 small martini glasses

1. Place 1 1/2 teaspoons of the coffee syrup in each glass.

2. Add 2 small scoops of ice cream and drizzle with sauce.

3. Pour 1 tablespoon of vodka over each and serve immediately.

123

cool
desserts

ice cream
roll

About 1 pint (1 recipe) cooked coffee ice cream (pg 120)
1 coffee jelly roll (page 115)
1 cup (double recipe) caramel coffee sauce (pg 33)
1/3 cup powdered sugar

1. Prepare the ice cream, but only freeze slightly. Prepare the jelly roll and wrap in a towel until ready to use.

2. Unroll the cake and lay it flat on plastic wrap. Spread the ice cream over it and roll back up.

3. Wrap tightly with plastic and freeze until hard.

4. Prepare a double recipe of the caramel coffee sauce and keep warm.

5. Cover the roll with powdered sugar and slice into 1-inch portions. Serve with the warm caramel sauce.

ice cream–coffee sundae party

Indulge your friends and yourself in these sophisticated sundae toppings.

FOR EACH 10-OUNCE SUNDAE

3 ounces espresso or strong coffee, sweetened to taste
2 scoops coffee ice cream (pgs 120–122)
2 tablespoons caramel coffee sauce (pg 33)
2 tablespoons coffee whipped cream (pg 27)
1 chocolate-covered coffee bean

TOPPINGS
1 tablespoon almond caramel praline, chopped (pg 27)
2 tablespoons caramelized coffee pecans, chopped (pg 28)
2 tablespoons chocolate-covered or candied macadamias, chopped

OPTIONAL
2 tablespoons coffee liqueur
2 tablespoons amaretto
2 tablespoons crème de cacao

1. Place coffee into a large cup or glass.
2. Add ice cream scoops and top with caramel coffee sauce and coffee whipped cream.
3. Sprinkle with toppings and decorate with a chocolate coffee bean.
4. Drizzle with liqueur, if desired.

mocha irish
coffee sundae

2 scoops mocha ice cream (pg 120, see variation)
3 ounces freshly brewed espresso or strong coffee, sweetened to taste
3 tablespoons coffee whipped cream (pg 27)
Chocolate-covered coffee beans
1 1/2 tablespoons Irish whisky
1 tablespoon *dulce de leche*

1. Place ice cream scoops in a large cup or heatproof glass. Pour the coffee over the ice cream.

2. Top with whipped cream and decorate with chocolate-covered coffee beans. Mix the whisky and *dulce de leche* together, and pour on top.

strawberries
with balsamic
sauce
over
ice cream

8 1/2-CUP SERVINGS

24 fresh (about 3 cups) strawberries whole, washed
1 cup (4 recipes) balsamic reduction sauce (pg 32)
2 tablespoons mint leaves, julienned
1 pint vanilla ice cream
1 pint coffee ice cream

1. Dry the strawberries with paper towels.

2. Prepare the balsamic reduction sauce, add the mint leaves, and set aside to cool.

3. Place a small scoop of vanilla ice cream in the bottom of a glass, and top with 1 strawberry and 1 tablespoon of sauce. Add a scoop of coffee ice cream, another strawberry, and another tablespoon of sauce.

126

cappuccino

mini cheesecakes

The cookie base, caramel coffee sauce, coffee–cream cheese filling, and airy whipped cream combine for a wonderfully rich flavor.

8 ounces cream cheese
3/4 cup sugar
2 tablespoons basic concentrated coffee (pg 36) or brewed espresso
1/4 teaspoon salt
1 tablespoon unflavored gelatin
1 tablespoon water
8 vanilla wafers or fantastic coffee and white chocolate chunk cookies (pg 71)
1/2 cup (1 recipe) caramel coffee sauce (pg 33, see variations below)
1/2 cup heavy cream
1/4 cup powdered sugar

8 2-inch aluminum rings, 3- to 4-inches tall*
Pastry bag with leaf or other decorative tip

1. Process the cream cheese and sugar in a food processor for 1 minute, or until you can no longer feel the sugar.

2. Add the coffee or espresso and salt, mix for 10 seconds more.

3. Cook gelatin and water in a small saucepan over low heat until the gelatin becomes liquid. Add to the processor while running and mix thoroughly. Transfer the mixture to a bowl and refrigerate for 3 to 5 minutes, just until cool.

4. Place 1 cookie at the bottom of each ring, press to cut off edges. Place the rings, with the cookies in them, on baking sheet.

5. Spread 1 tablespoon of the caramel coffee sauce over each cookie, then add 1/3 cup of the cheesecake mixture to each ring. (Using an ice cream scoop makes this easier.) Freeze for 45 minutes, then transfer to the refrigerator.

6. When ready to serve, press the cookie up from the bottom to loosen it and then push all the way through. Set each one on a serving plate. The coffee sauce will ooze out, but the cheesecake will hold perfectly.

7. Beat the cream and sugar on high speed for 1 1/2 to 2 minutes, or until stiff peaks form. Transfer to a pastry bag with a decorative tip, and top each cheesecake with whipped cream.

8. Serve immediately or keep refrigerated until ready to serve.

VARIATIONS: Omit the caramel coffee sauce from step 5, and serve it directly on the plate if desired. If you want the sauce to stiffen like the cheesecake, blend 1 teaspoon unflavored gelatin with 1 teaspoon water and add this to the recipe while preparing the sauce. Cool before adding it to the cookie.

*This can also be prepared in a 6-inch round springform pan or ring lined with foil.

chocolate chip

mocha cheesecake

This divine recipe is one of my favorites! It makes for a beautiful presentation!

CRUST

22 Oreo cookies

4 tablespoons (1/2 stick) butter, softened

3 tablespoons brewed espresso or 1 tablespoon concentrated coffee syrup (pgs 36–37)

FILLING

24 ounces cream cheese

1 cup ricotta cheese

1 1/2 cups granulated sugar

3 tablespoons all-purpose flour

1 tablespoon unsweetened cocoa

2 tablespoons freeze-dried or granulated instant coffee

1 tablespoon coffee liqueur (such as Kahlua)

3 eggs

1/2 cup chocolate chips

8-inch cheesecake mold or springform pan

1. Preheat the oven to 300°F. Cover bottom of the pan with aluminum foil (do not butter or flour).

2. Process cookies into crumbs with a food processor, about 1 minute. Add the butter and espresso or coffee syrup and process for 5 to 7 seconds, or until all of the butter has been absorbed. Pour into the pan and spread evenly, pressing and flattening with your fingertips. Set aside.

3. Process the cream cheese, ricotta, and sugar in a clean food processor for 2 to 3 minutes, or until you can no longer feel the sugar. Add the flour and cocoa, and mix.

4. Mix the coffee and liqueur in a small bowl and add to the processor. Add the eggs and process for 10 seconds more, until just blended.

5. Mix in the chocolate chips by hand and pour into the pan on top of the crust.

6. Set the pan on a baking sheet and bake for 1 hour and 30 minutes. Set aside to cool. Refrigerate for 2 hours or more before serving.

129

cool desserts

rum and coffee

cheesecake

Cheesecakes are the most rewarding desserts: they are simple to make, easy to store, and taste delicious. You can freeze these and serve them individually, or cut them into bite-size triangles for a party or buffet.

CRUST
12 (1/3 recipe) crispy speckled white chocolate chip coffee cookies (pg 67) or 25 graham cracker squares
4 tablespoons (1/2 stick) butter
1 tablespoon basic concentrated coffee (pg 36) or brewed espresso

FILLING
1 pound cream cheese (2 8-ounce blocks)
1 cup sugar
3 tablespoons all-purpose flour
2 eggs
2 tablespoons freeze-dried or granulated instant coffee
1/4 cup dark rum
1/2 cup sour cream

CARAMEL ALMOND TOPPING
1/2 cup sliced almonds
1/4 cup light brown sugar
2 tablespoons butter, cut into pea-sized pieces
2 tablespoons dark rum

4 4-inch cheesecake molds or springform pans

1. Preheat the oven to 300°F. Cover bottoms of the pans with aluminum foil (do not butter or flour).

2. Process the cookies or graham crackers into crumbs in a food processor, about 1 minute. (Yields about 1 3/4 cups crumbs.) Add the butter and coffee or espresso and process for 5 to 7 seconds, or until all of the butter has been absorbed. Divide into 4 parts and place into the bottoms of the molds. Spread and flatten with your fingertips. Set aside.

3. Process the cheese and sugar in a clean food processor for 2 to 3 minutes, until you can no longer feel the sugar. Add the flour and mix.

4. With the processor running, add the eggs. Mix the coffee with the rum in a small bowl, pour into the processor. Add the sour cream, and mix 5 to 10 seconds more.

5. Pour into the pans on top of the crusts. Set the pans on a baking sheet. Bake for 45 minutes. Set aside to cool (do not turn off the oven) and refrigerate for 1 hour or more.

6. While the cakes are cooling, prepare the topping. Place the almonds in a small baking pan, and sprinkle with the sugar and butter. Bake for 20 minutes. Remove from the oven, drizzle with the rum, and place back in the oven for 5 to 8 minutes more. Set aside to cool.

7. Remove the cakes from the pans and sprinkle with the almonds. Serve as individual cakes or cut into mini triangles (12 wedges per cake).

mocha
cheesecake

cups over
nougatine

This simple but impressive dessert is perfect for the beginner cook. The sauce oozes as you spoon out the cheesecake—they are mouthwatering!

1 cup chopped toasted pecans (see tips, pgs 38–39)
1 1/2 cups sugar (divided use)
1/4 cup water
4 ounces cream cheese
4 eggs
3/4 cups milk
1 1/2 teaspoons freeze-dried or granulated instant coffee
1 teaspoon vanilla extract
1 recipe caramelized coffee pecans (pg 28), optional

8 3-inch ramekins

1. Preheat the oven to 350°F. Divide the toasted pecans into eight portions, set aside.

2. To prepare a caramel for the bottom of the ramekins, place 3/4 cup of the sugar and the water in a small, heavy saucepan over high heat. Once it begins to boil, decrease heat to medium and cook for 5 to 7 minutes, or until lightly golden. Immediately pour the caramel into the ramekins to cover the bottoms. (The caramel is very hot, so wear gloves.) Set aside.

3. Process the cream cheese and remaining 3/4 cup sugar in a food processor for 1 1/2 minutes. Add the eggs, milk, coffee, and vanilla extract and mix for 1 minute. Pour mixture into ramekins.

4. Set ramekins into a baking pan and pour surround with 1 inch of water. Place into the oven and immediately decrease the oven temperature to 250°F. Bake for 55 to 60 minutes.

5. Remove from oven, and remove ramekins from outer pan. Set aside to cool. Refrigerate until completely cold.

6. Serve decorated with caramelized pecans, if desired.

mamina's coffee mousse

with mocha-rum sauce

My mother created the recipe for this delicious coffee mousse. She sold it at the bakery she had for more than thirty years. The sauce can be used in many other recipes like the white chocolate–coffee mousse (pg 137) or served over waffles, French toast, or ice cream.

1 8-INCH BOWL, 10 TO 12 SERVINGS

4 eggs, separated
1 3/4 cups sugar (divided use)
2/3 cup water
4 tablespoons freeze-dried or granulated instant coffee
3 tablespoons unflavored gelatin
2 cups heavy cream, very cold
1 teaspoon vanilla extract
1/2 teaspoon cream of tartar
3/4 cup (1 recipe) mocha-rum sauce (pg 34)

1. Beat the egg yolks and 1 cup of the sugar in an electric mixer at medium speed for 8 to 10 minutes, or until the mixture looks white and creamy like mayonnaise.

2. Mix the water, coffee, and gelatin in a small saucepan. Stir over medium-low heat to dissolve (do not boil). Remove from the heat and set aside. Pour into the yolk mixture and mix until absorbed, about 1 minute.

3. Transfer to a shallow pan and freeze 10 to 15 minutes, until completely set. When set, puree the mixture in a food processor or blender.

4. Beat the cream in a clean, dry bowl at high speed for 1 1/2 to 2 minutes, or until stiff. Add the vanilla extract. Fold in the puree.

5. In a clean mixer bowl, beat the egg whites and cream of tartar with clean beaters at medium-high speed for 1 minute, or until foamy. Add the remaining 3/4 cup sugar a tablespoon at a time, and continue mixing for 2 minutes, or until soft peaks form. Fold some of the whites into the cream mixture, and then fold it back into the rest of the whites.

6. Lightly spray an 8-inch glass or stainless-steel bowl with nonstick oil. Pour in the mousse mixture and freeze or refrigerate until set.

7. When set, pass the tip of a knife around the sides of the mousse and then set over very hot water for 2 to 3 minutes. Turn over on a serving dish and serve with mocha-rum sauce.

133

cool desserts

caramel

coffee

mousse

2 cups granulated sugar (divided use)
1 cup water
6 egg whites
Pinch of salt
1 1/2 cups powdered sugar
2 tablespoons amaretto-flavored freeze-dried or granulated instant coffee
1 tablespoon coffee liqueur
1/2 teaspoon vanilla extract or 1 teaspoon vanilla sugar (see tips, pgs 38–39)
1 1/2 cups (1 recipe) coffee crème anglaise sauce, chilled

1. To prepare a caramel, place 1 1/2 cups of the granulated sugar and the water in a small, heavy saucepan over high heat. Once it begins to boil, decrease heat to medium and cook for 7 to 10 minutes, or until lightly golden. Immediately pour into a 8- to 9-inch heatproof glass or stainless steel bowl. Swirl to cover the entire inside surface of the bowl. (The caramel is very hot, so wear gloves.) Set aside.

2. Preheat the oven to 325°F.

3. In a clean mixer bowl, beat the egg whites and salt on medium speed for 1 to 2 minutes, or until foamy. Slowly add the powdered sugar, and mix for 6 minutes more.

4. Place the remaining 1/2 cup granulated sugar in a small skillet or saucepan over medium heat. Without stirring, let it melt and caramelize, until lightly golden. Carefully pour it in a thin stream into the whites and mix for 2 minutes more.

5. Mix the coffee, liqueur, and vanilla extract in a small bowl. Add to the mixer bowl and mix.

6. Transfer the mixture to the caramel-lined bowl. With a spatula, try to remove all of the air bubbles. (A glass bowl is helpful here since it allows you to clearly see if any air bubbles are along the side.)

7. Place bowl into a baking dish and surround with 1 inch of water. Bake for 1 hour.

8. Remove from oven, and remove bowl from outer pan. Set aside until it reaches room temperature (can sit overnight).

9. To loosen the caramel, pour about 2 to 3 tablespoons of water along the edge of the bowl, between the mousse and the caramel. Swirl the bowl until the mousse has completely loosened, and then turn it upside down on a deep serving dish. Spoon any caramel that oozes out back over the mousse.

10. Serve in pretty dessert dishes topped with coffee crème anglaise sauce.

passion fruit
and coffee
mousse

18 (1/2 recipe) ladyfingers (pg 72)
1/2 cup (1 recipe) caramel coffee sauce (pg 33)
1 1/4 cups passion fruit pulp (from 3/4 pound fruit; see tips, pgs 38–39)
1 1/4 cups sugar (divided use)
2 tablespoons unflavored gelatin
2 tablespoons water
1 1/2 cups heavy cream
2 egg whites

1 charlotte mold or 1 deep 8-inch cheesecake mold

1. Prepare the ladyfingers and let cool. Prepare the caramel coffee sauce. Line the mold with foil.

2. Mix the passion fruit pulp and 3/4 cup of the sugar in a medium bowl with a whisk.

3. Place the gelatin and water in a small saucepan. Cook over low heat to melt the gelatin. Add to the pulp and mix thoroughly.

4. Pour the mixture into a rectangular pan and freeze until set, about 20 minutes. Remove from the freezer and transfer to a food processor. Process until smooth.

5. Beat the heavy cream in an electric mixer on high speed until soft peaks form. Fold into the passion fruit mixture.

6. In a clean mixer bowl, beat the egg whites with clean beaters on high speed until foamy, about 2 minutes. Slowly add the remaining 1/2 cup sugar and beat to stiff peaks, about 3 minutes more. Add some of the whites to the passion fruit–cream mixture and then fold into the rest of the whites.

7. Arrange the ladyfingers around the sides of the mold. Pour the mousse into the center of the ladyfingers and refrigerate to set, about 10 minutes.

8. Remove the mousse from the refrigerator and pour the caramel coffee sauce in circles over the top of the mousse. Lightly swirl the sauce into the mousse with a fork or a wooden skewer.

9. Refrigerate until set (or overnight), or freeze for about 2 hours. Turn upside down onto a serving plate, peel off the foil, and serve.

135

cool
desserts

mocha

mousse

cups

This is possibly the easiest mousse recipe you will ever find. I have noticed that men are particularly fond of it. It keeps well in the refrigerator for 3 or 4 days covered with plastic wrap.

6 SERVINGS

KAHLUA SYRUP
1/3 cup water
2 teaspoons freeze-dried or granulated instant coffee
2 tablespoons sugar
1 teaspoon unflavored gelatin
2 tablespoons Kahlua

MOUSSE
2 eggs, separated
1 tablespoon Kahlua
1 1/2 cups chocolate chips (3/4 of a 12-ounce package)
3 tablespoons heavy cream
1 tablespoon freeze-dried or granulated instant coffee
1/2 cup sugar
1/4 teaspoon cream of tartar

White chocolate block, for shavings (see tips, pgs 38–39)
Champagne flutes

1. To prepare the syrup, combine the water and coffee in a small saucepan. Mix in the sugar and gelatin and bring to a boil over medium-low heat. Stir well and immediately remove from the heat. Stir in 2 tablespoons of Kahlua. Divide the syrup among 6 champagne flutes, and refrigerate until the mousse is ready.

2. Mix egg yolks and 1 tablespoon of Kahlua in a small bowl and set aside for 15 minutes.

2. Chop the chocolate chips in a food processor, pulsing about 10 times.

3. Place the cream in a large glass bowl and microwave on high for 30 seconds. Stir in the yolk-Kahlua mixture and coffee. Add to the food processor, and process until smooth and not so hot, about 2 minutes. Refrigerate to cool.

4. Beat the egg whites and cream of tartar in a clean mixer bowl at medium-high speed for 1 minute, or until foamy. Add the sugar 1 tablespoon at a time and beat for 3 minutes more, or until stiff peaks form.

5. Fold some of the whites into the chocolate and then fold it back into the remaining whites.

6. Pour the mousse gently into the glasses over the syrup and refrigerate to set, about 30 minutes.

7. Shave some white chocolate into each glass and serve with a long spoon.

white chocolate– coffee
mousse
and shots

This is an adaptation of a chocolate mousse from the famous Lenôtre school in Paris. It is a delicate mousse with a hint of coffee. This would be great to serve next to the fireplace on a cold winter night, with a glass of coffee and liqueur cream.

6 tablespoons sugar
6 tablespoons water (divided use)
1 tablespoon freeze-dried or granulated instant coffee
1 tablespoon coffee liqueur
4 tablespoons (1/2 stick) butter
5 ounces white chocolate, chopped (plus 1 ounce more for shavings)
2 egg whites
1/4 teaspoon cream of tartar
1/8 teaspoon salt
1/4 cup concentrated coffee syrup (pgs 36–37)
Whole coffee beans, optional

8 3- to 4-ounce shot glasses
Pastry bag with coupler only or large plain tip

1. To make a syrup, bring the sugar and 4 tablespoons of the water to a boil in a small saucepan, reduce the heat to medium, and simmer for 3 minutes. Mix the remaining 2 tablespoons of water with the coffee, and add to the saucepan (be careful, coffee boils high), and simmer for 1 minute more. Remove from the heat, cool, and stir in the liqueur.

2. Cream the butter in an electric mixer on medium speed for 4 minutes, or until soft and shiny. Add half of the syrup in a steady stream and beat for 3 minutes more.

3. Place the chocolate in a large glass bowl and microwave on high for 25 seconds, mix with a fork, and set aside.

4. In a clean mixer bowl, beat the egg whites, cream of tartar, and salt with clean beaters on medium-high speed until frothy, about 2 minutes. Slowly add the remaining syrup, and beat on high speed for 8 minutes, until shiny and thick.

5. Fold the whites into the chocolate, and then fold this mixture into the creamed butter. Pour into a pastry bag and refrigerate until ready to use. (If using the mousse for another recipe, proceed with the directions for that recipe.)

6. To make mousse shots, pour a teaspoon of concentrated coffee syrup in the bottom of each shot glass. Pipe out the mousse over the syrup. Add another teaspoon of syrup over the mousse. Decorate with white chocolate shavings or a single coffee bean.

137

cool
desserts

bombe with white chocolate– coffee mousse

Make this dessert when you want to show off!

1 8-inch bowl (1/2 recipe) vanilla-and-coffee-dotted chiffon cake (pg 112)
3 tablespoons sugar
3 tablespoons water
2 tablespoons vodka
1 tablespoons freeze-dried or granulated instant coffee
3 cups (1 recipe) white chocolate–coffee mousse (pg 137)
2/3 cup (1 recipe) dark chocolate ganache (pg 28)
3 ounces coverture chocolate, for decoration

1. The day before, prepare the chiffon cake and allow to cool.

2. To prepare a syrup, bring the sugar and water to a boil in a small saucepan, reduce the heat to medium, simmer for 3 minutes, and remove from the heat. Mix the vodka with the coffee in a small bowl and add to the syrup. Set aside to cool.*

3. When you are ready to assemble the dessert, prepare the white chocolate–coffee mousse and ganache.

4. Turn the cake bowl upside down onto a platter, remove the cake, peel off the foil, and return the foil to the bowl. Cut a 3/4-inch slice from the wide, flat bottom of the cake and set aside. Return the rest of the cake to the bowl.

5. Scoop out the cake interior with a spoon to create an empty dome. Brush the inside of the cake dome with half of the syrup. Fill with the coffee mousse and replace the cake bottom. Brush with the remaining syrup and refrigerate about 4 hours, or freeze for 1 hour.

6. Using the coverture chocolate, prepare chocolate leaves for decoration (see tips, pgs 38–39).

7. Place a serving plate on top of the bowl, invert the plate and bowl, and lift the bowl off the cake. Discard the foil. Frost with the ganache and decorate with chocolate leaves.

*The syrup can be prepared the day before.

white chocolate and coffee berry mousse cups

These cups are beautiful, rich, heartwarming, and delicate. For true elegance on a very special occasion, serve them in champagne flutes.

12 SERVINGS

3 cups (1 recipe) white chocolate–coffee mousse (see pg 137)
1 1/2 cups red raspberries
1/2 cup brewed coffee, hot
2 tablespoons sugar
2 tablespoons heavy cream
1/2 teaspoon unflavored gelatin
3 tablespoons cognac (divided use)
1/2 cup (1 recipe) caramel coffee sauce (pg 33)

12 champagne flutes, wine glasses, or ramekins

1. Prepare the mousse. Reserve 12 raspberries and gently fold the rest into the mousse. Refrigerate until set.

2. To prepare the coffee gelatin, combine the coffee, sugar, cream, and gelatin in a small saucepan. Heat just to dissolve the gelatin and remove from the heat. Stir in 1 tablespoon of the cognac.

3. Pour about 1 tablespoon of the gelatin into the bottom of each serving glass. Refrigerate for 5 minutes to thicken slightly.

4. Add the mousse to the glasses on top of the coffee gelatin. Refrigerate to set, about 1 hour.

5. Prepare the caramel coffee sauce, remove from the heat, and add the remaining 2 tablespoons cognac. Stir to mix and return to the heat to cook off some alcohol, about 1 minute. Refrigerate to cool.

6. Pour 2 teaspoons of the caramel coffee sauce over each mousse and top with a raspberry.

coffee
crème

charlotte

1 cup (1/2 recipe) coffee pastry cream (pg 30)
4 teaspoons unflavored gelatin
1 1/2 tablespoons water
1/2 cup heavy cream, very cold
1/4 cup powdered sugar
1 teaspoon cognac
1 tablespoon concentrated coffee syrup (pgs 36–37)

1. Prepare the pastry cream and set aside. (Do not cool.)

2. Mix the gelatin and water in a small saucepan and gently heat to dissolve the gelatin. Pour into the warm pastry cream and mix well. Refrigerate or place in an ice bath to cool.

3. Beat the heavy cream in an electric mixer on high speed for 1 to 2 minutes, or until slightly thickened. Add the powdered sugar and cognac and mix 30 seconds to 1 minute more, until it holds its shape. Be careful not to overmix.

4. Whisk the cooled pastry cream until smooth. Fold some of the whipped cream into the pastry cream, and then fold this back into the remaining whipped cream. (If the pastry cream has gelled too much and is too stiff to fold with the cream, briefly mix it in a food processor until softened again.)

5. Keep cold until ready to use.

coffee
charlotte

You can also serve this dessert with the yellow gooseberry sauce (pg 35) or the white chocolate–coffee sauce (pg 35).

4 1/2 cups (3 recipes) coffee crème charlotte (pg 140)
18 (1/2 recipe) ladyfingers (pg 72)
2 ounces chocolate
Berries, optional

1 6-inch charlotte mold or deep cake pan

1. Prepare the coffee crème charlotte. Prepare the ladyfingers. Allow to cool and set aside. (These can be prepared a day ahead.)

2. Lightly butter the bottom and sides of the mold or spray with nonstick oil. Place the ladyfingers along the edge of the mold.

3. Fill with the coffee crème charlotte and cover with plastic wrap or waxed paper.

4. Refrigerate until set, preferably overnight, or freeze for 1 to 2 hours.

5. Turn upside down onto on a serving platter and remove the pan.

6. Melt the chocolate in a small glass bowl in the microwave and spread over 2 4-inch pieces of waxed paper. Wrap them around paper cups, hold with some tape, and freeze for 5 minutes. Remove from the freezer and peel off the paper.

7. Place the chocolate curls on top of the charlotte. Decorate with berries, if desired.

crêpe

tower

8 SMALL SERVINGS

24 (double recipe) basic crêpes (pg 24)
1 cup (double recipe) caramel coffee sauce (pg 33)
2/3 cup (1 recipe) white chocolate ganache (pg 28)
2/3 cup (1 recipe) dark chocolate ganache (pg 28)
Powdered sugar
6 large strawberries, sliced
3/4 cups (1 recipe) mocha-rum sauce (pg 34)

1. Place a crêpe on a plate or serving dish. Spread with caramel coffee sauce. Cover with another crêpe and spread with white chocolate ganache. Cover with another crêpe and spread with dark chocolate ganache.

2. Repeat until all of the crêpes have been used.

3. Cover tightly with plastic wrap and refrigerate for 30 minutes, or until firm enough to cut. Divide into 6 portions.

4. Serve sprinkled with powdered sugar, strawberry slices, and with the mocha-rum sauce on the side.

TIP: To help aid spreading, drizzle the ganache over the crêpes with a plastic or pastry bag (see tips, pgs 38–39) and then spread, or just cover with the next crêpe.

coffee crème

caramel

Delicious and super-simple to make, this dessert is great when prepared one or even two days ahead and kept refrigerated in its baking pan.

passion
for
coffee

10 TO 12 SERVINGS

2 cups sugar (divided use)
1 cup water
4 cups milk
3 tablespoons amaretto-flavored freeze-dried or granulated instant coffee
4 eggs
4 egg yolks
1/2 teaspoon vanilla extract or 1 teaspoon vanilla sugar (see tips, pgs 38–39)

1. Preheat the oven to 350°F.

2. To prepare a caramel, place 1 cup of the sugar and the water in a small, heavy saucepan over high heat. Once it begins to boil, decrease heat to medium and cook for 7 to 10 minutes, or until lightly golden. Immediately pour into a 10-inch round cake pan. Swirl to cover the entire surface of the pan. (The caramel is very hot, so wear gloves.) Set aside.

3. Bring the milk, remaining 1 cup of sugar, and coffee to a boil in a saucepan over medium-high heat. Meanwhile, lightly beat the eggs with the egg yolks. Remove the milk mixture from the heat, and whisk in the beaten eggs until completely incorporated, about 1 minute. Mix in the vanilla extract or vanilla sugar. Pass through a sieve into the caramel-lined pan.

4. Set the pan into a baking dish and surround with 1 inch of water. Bake for 1 hour and 30 minutes, or until set in the middle.

5. Remove from the oven. Remove the cake pan from the outer pan and et aside to cool. Refrigerate, preferably overnight.

6. When ready to serve, pass a knife around the sides to help release it. Swirl the cake pan to make sure it has released completely. Place your serving dish upside down over the pan and quickly flip the whole thing over. Remove the pan. Serve cold.

VARIATION: You can also make this in 3-inch ramekins. Cook these at 375°F for 30 minutes (18 servings).

dulce *de leche*

and coffee natilla

Natilla is the traditional dessert for Christmas in the Andean region of Colombia. Nowadays, it is prepared with many flavors, but this is the first recipe I know of that uses coffee. Enjoy this not-too-sweet pudding, that is easy to serve and store.

4 cups whole milk (divided use)
1/2 cup firmly packed dark brown sugar
2 tablespoons freeze-dried or granulated instant coffee
2 cinnamon sticks
1/4 teaspoon baking soda
1/8 teaspoon salt
1 cup cornstarch
1/2 cup *dulce de leche*, plus extra for garnishing
Ground cinnamon and whole coffee beans, for garnishing

1. This dessert is prepared directly into individual serving dishes or a decorative bowl. If you wish to serve cut pieces instead, lightly spray a mold or an 8-inch pan (square or round) with nonstick cooking oil to aid in removing the dessert onto a serving platter after it is set.

2. Place 3 cups of the milk, brown sugar, coffee, cinnamon sticks, baking soda, and salt in a medium, heavy saucepan over medium-low heat. Simmer, stirring for 3 to 5 minutes or until the brown sugar has completely dissolved. Do not let the mixture boil.

3. In a small bowl, stir the remaining 1 cup milk and the cornstarch until completely dissolved. Add to the saucepan and mix.

4. Raise the heat to medium and stir vigorously once it begins to boil. Scraping the bottom of the pan, cook until the mixture has thickened and you can see the bottom of the pan when you stir, about 5 to 7 minutes.

5. Remove the pan from heat, add the *dulce de leche*, and mix well. Remove the cinnamon sticks.

6. Immediately pour into a serving dish or the prepared mold. Sprinkle with ground cinnamon, and decorate with drops of *dulce de leche* and coffee beans. Refrigerate until set.

hot and cold drinks

From *tinto*, the traditional black coffee of Colombia, to the now ultra-popular Italian *cappuccino*, these drinks satisfy a variety of tastes at any time of the day. *Café con leche*—or *latté*—is our breakfast coffee drink of choice, but it's good whenever you're craving a simple but satisfying warm coffee drink. Regular and low-calorie frozen coffee drinks cool you down and give you energy on hot days, and spiced or spiked coffees are perfect after dinner or as nightcaps.

black

coffee (*tinto*)

One of the most common coffee drinks in Latin American countries is *tinto*, a 2- to 3-ounce cup of smooth, black, warm coffee. The Colombian Coffee Federation suggests brewing 2 tablespoons of ground coffee for every 6 ounces of water.

1 1/4 CUPS (10 OUNCES), ABOUT 3 TO 4 SERVINGS

1/4 cup (4 tablespoons) ground coffee
1 1/2 cups (12 ounces) cold water
Sugar, optional

Place the coffee in the filter of a drip coffee maker. Add the water to the machine. Turn on and brew. Sweeten, if desired.

classic cafe con leche

or *café latté*

Our favorite breakfast drink is always made with hot or warm milk. It wakes up adults as well as children in Columbia every day!

2 8-OUNCE SERVINGS

1/4 cup ground coffee
1 cup cold water
1 1/4 cups warm milk*
Sugar, optional

Brew the coffee with the water. Heat the milk in a microwave or on the stovetop. (Make sure to remove any skin that may form on the surface of the milk.) Serve 3 ounces of coffee in a mug or cup and add the warm milk. Sweeten, if desired.

VARIATION: For a café mocha, add 1/2 ounce dark or milk chocolate shavings.

*You can use skim, 2%, or whole milk. With skim milk, you may want to add an extra 1/4 cup of milk so that the coffee is not too strong.

cappuccino

This is a new drink for Latin American countries, and it has taken our major cities by storm. For the best *cappuccino* possible, you need two things: fresh coffee (whole bean or freshly ground) and an espresso machine with strong pressure for making frothy milk and a creamy, full-bodied espresso. The perfect *cappuccino* should be 1/3 espresso, 1/3 milk, and 1/3 milk foam, according to professional coffee baristas.

Before you add the coffee to the machine, have all of the ingredients ready, including the cup. Froth the milk immediately after turning on the machine and add it to the coffee as soon as possible—do not let the coffee sit.

For a different flavor, add 1 1/2 teaspoons of Grand Marnier or cognac, or 1 tablespoon of crème de cacao or amaretto.

frozen coffee frappes

Drinking a frappe is one of my favorite ways to cool off! Store some coffee syrup in the fridge—it keeps for up to a week—and enjoy these cold, icy drinks anytime.

1 12-OUNCE SERVING

Blend all the ingredients and serve in a tall glass.

coffee
2 tablespoons sweet coffee syrup for drinks (pg 37)
1/4 cup evaporated milk
1/4 cup 2% milk
1 tablespoon dark brown sugar
1 cup crushed ice

mocha
1 tablespoon sweet coffee syrup for drinks (pg 37)
1/4 cup evaporated milk
1/4 cup milk
2 tablespoons dark brown sugar
2 tablespoons dark chocolate ganache (pg 28)
1 cup crushed ice

white chocolate
1 tablespoon sweet coffee syrup for drinks (pg 37)
1/4 cup evaporated milk
1/4 cup 2% milk
1 tablespoon dark brown sugar
2 tablespoons white chocolate ganache (pg 28)
1 cup crushed ice

caramel
2 tablespoons sweet coffee syrup for drinks (pg 37)
1/4 cup evaporated milk
1/4 cup 2% milk
2 tablespoon caramel coffee sauce (pg 33)
1 cup crushed ice

cookie
1 tablespoon sweet coffee syrup for drinks (pg 37)
1/4 cup evaporated milk
1/4 cup 2% milk
1 tablespoon dark brown sugar
2 Oreo cookies, crushed
1/4 teaspoon vanilla extract
1 cup crushed ice

frozen coffee

frappes (low-calorie)

These are guilt-free versions of the frappes—they have only 100 to 200 calories! I used Splenda, but you can use your favorite brand of sweetener.

1 12-OUNCE SERVING

Blend all the ingredients and serve in a tall glass.

coffee

1 1/4 teaspoons freeze-dried instant coffee
1/4 cup fat-free evaporated milk
1/4 cup 2% milk
2 packets artificial sweetener
1/2 teaspoon vanilla extract
1 cup crushed ice

mocha

1 1/2 teaspoons Irish coffee-flavored freeze-dried instant coffee
1/4 cup fat-free evaporated milk
1/4 cup 2% milk
3 packets artificial sweetener
1 1/2 teaspoons unsweetened cocoa
1 cup crushed ice

white chocolate

1 1/2 teaspoons macadamia-flavored freeze-dried instant coffee
1/4 cup fat-free evaporated milk
1/4 cup skim milk
1 packet artificial sweetener
1 ounce white chocolate shavings (see tips, pgs 38–39)
1 cup crushed ice

caramel

1 1/2 teaspoons amaretto-flavored freeze-dried instant coffee
1/4 cup fat-free evaporated milk
1/4 cup skim milk
2 packets artificial sweetener
1 tablespoon caramel almond topping (see rum and coffee cheesecake, pg 131) or spiced caramelized almonds (pg 28)
1 cup crushed ice

cookie

1 1/4 teaspoons vanilla-flavored freeze-dried instant coffee
1/4 cup fat-free evaporated milk
1/4 cup 2% milk
2 packets artificial sweetener
2 Oreo cookies, crushed
1/2 teaspoon vanilla extract
1 cup crushed ice

milk shakes

These rich and creamy milk shakes will make you feel like a kid again.

dulce de leche shake
1 12-OUNCE SERVING

1/2 cup milk
1 tablespoon sugar
1 1/2 teaspoons freeze-dried instant coffee
1 tablespoon *dulce de leche*
2 scoops coffee ice cream (pgs 120–122)
1 tablespoon whipped cream

Blender

Mix the milk, sugar, and coffee in a blender until the sugar dissolves. Place the *dulce de leche* at the bottom of a tall glass. Add one scoop of ice cream to the blender, mix, and pour into the glass. Add the other ice cream scoop to the glass and top with whipped cream.

mocha milk shake
1 12-OUNCE SERVING

1/2 cup milk
2 tablespoons sugar
1 1/2 teaspoons freeze-dried instant coffee
2 tablespoons chocolate sauce
2 ounces dark chocolate, grated
2 scoops coffee ice cream (pgs 120–122) or mocha ice cream (see variation, pg 120)
1 cherry, for decoration

Blender

Combine the milk, sugar, and coffee in a saucepan and heat for 1 to 2 minutes, until the milk is hot and the sugar has dissolved. Remove from heat and cool to room temperature. Place the chocolate sauce at the bottom of a tall glass. Mix the milk mixture in a blender with the grated chocolate and one scoop of the ice cream. Cool the mixture completely by placing it over a bowl of ice, and pour into the glass. Add the other scoop of ice cream to the glass and decorate with a cherry.

*You may use store-bought sauce or the dark chocolate sauce (pg 34) from this book.

spiced black coffee

Serve these hot and spicy drinks in your nicest cups with elegant sweets.

1/4 cup ground coffee
Spice (ground allspice, grated nutmeg, aniseed, cinnamon sticks, cloves)
1 1/2 cups cold water
Sugar, optional

allspice-nutmeg spiced coffee

Place the coffee, **1/4 teaspoon ground allspice**, and **1/8 teaspoon freshly grated nutmeg** in the filter of a coffee maker. Brew with the water and serve. Sweeten, if desired.

aniseed spiced coffee

Place **1/8 teaspoon toasted aniseeds** (see tips, pgs 38–39) directly into the coffee pot of a coffee maker. Place the coffee in the filter and brew with the water. Allow the coffee to sit for 3 to 5 minutes and pass through a sieve to serve. Sweeten, if desired.

cinnamon spiced coffee

Place the coffee and **2 1/2-inch pieces of cinnamon stick** in the filter of a coffee maker. Place **2 cinnamon sticks** into the coffee pot. Brew with the water, allow the coffee to sit for 5 minutes, and pass through a sieve to serve. Place **1 long cinnamon stick** into each cup to use as a stirrer. Sweeten, if desired.

cloves-nutmeg spiced coffee

Place the coffee and **5 whole cloves** in the filter of a coffee maker. Place **5 whole cloves** into the coffee pot. Brew with the water, allow the coffee to sit for 5 minutes, and pass through a sieve to serve. Add **less than a pinch of nutmeg** into each cup. Sweeten, if desired.

spiced café con leche

or spiced café latté

Spiced coffee with milk soothes and energizes, and can help you to feel better when you're under the weather.

1/4 cup ground coffee
Spice (cinnamon sticks, allspice berries, cloves, vanilla beans, grated nutmeg)
1 cup cold water
1/3 to 1 cup milk*
Sugar, optional
1 recipe herbed or spiced basic simple syrup (see variation, pg 36), optional

cinnamon-allspice *café con leche*

Place the coffee and **2 1/2-inch pieces cinnamon stick** in the filter of a coffee maker and brew with the water. Bring **1 cinnamon stick, 6 cracked allspice berries**, and the milk to a boil in a saucepan, immediately turn down the heat, and simmer for 5 minutes. Pour the coffee into 2 cups and pass the milk through a sieve into the coffee to serve. Sweeten with sugar or syrup, if desired.

cinnamon-cloves *café con leche*

Place the coffee and **2 1/2-inch pieces cinnamon stick** in the filter of a coffee maker and brew with the water. Bring **1 cinnamon stick, 5 cloves**, and the milk to a boil in a saucepan, immediately turn down the heat, and simmer for 5 minutes. Pour the coffee into 2 cups and pass the milk through a sieve into the coffee to serve. Sweeten with sugar or syrup, if desired.

vanilla-nutmeg *café con leche*

Place the coffee in the filter of a coffee maker and brew with the water. Bring **1/4 of a split vanilla bean**, a **pinch of nutmeg**, and the milk to a boil in a saucepan, immediately turn down the heat, and simmer for 5 minutes. Pour the coffee into 2 cups and pass the milk through a sieve into the coffee to serve. Sweeten with sugar or syrup, if desired. (To reuse the vanilla bean, wash and dry it thoroughly.)

*Use 1/3 cup of milk for a darker drink, and 1 cup for lighter one. I usually prepare the whole cup of milk and refrigerate the rest for future drinks.

cold

café latté

Cold lattés are a great way to use leftover coffee. Refrigerate your leftover strong coffee immediately, then enjoy a cool refreshing drink later after a hot or exhausting day.

2 12-OUNCE SERVINGS

1/4 cup ground coffee
2 cups cold water
1 cup milk*
Sugar, optional

Place the coffee in the filter of a coffee maker. Brew using 1 cup of the water. Add the remaining cold water and milk and cool completely. Pour into a 12-ounce glass full of ice and serve. Sweeten, if desired.

VARIATION: For a cold mocha latté, add 1/2 ounce of melted chocolate to the brewed coffee and mix well with a wire whisk.

*You can use skim, 2%, or whole milk.

spicy

macchiatos

A warm macchiato, literally meaning "marked espresso," is best enjoyed on a cold winter afternoon by eating the milk foam with a spoon, and then slowly enjoying every sip. Have fun forming designs with the milk foam when serving!

2 SERVINGS

1 1/2 cups spiced milk (see spiced *café con leche*, pg 155)
Sugar, optional
1 recipe herbed or spiced basic simple syrup (see variation, pg 36), optional
2 1-ounce espresso shots

Cappuccino maker (with milk steamer)

Prepare the spiced milk of your choice using 1 1/2 cups of milk. Sweeten with sugar or syrup, if desired, and keep cold. Brew espresso shots. When ready to serve, steam the milk and tap it lightly to remove large air bubbles. Serve one espresso shot in each of two tall, heatproof glasses. Slowly pour in the milk. As you reach the top of the glass, use the thin stream of milk to "mark" the drink by making a design in the foam, such as a heart or a streak.

VARIATIONS: Add 1/4 teaspoon almond extract or 1 teaspoon amaretto for an almond macchiato; or 1/4 ounce melted chocolate for a mocha macchiato.

spiked
coffees

These drinks are the most fun of all—
there's one for each part of the day!

1/3 cup ground coffee
1 1/2 cups cold water
Sugar, optional

Brew the coffee with the water. Sweeten, if desired. Pour 3 ounces of the coffee into each of 3 serving glasses or mugs.

cappuccino-style mocha coffee

Froth **2 cups milk**. Add **2 tablespoons crème de cacao** to each serving. Pour 6 ounces of the milk into each. Garnish with **powdered cocoa**.

cognac evening coffee

Add **1 1/2 teaspoons cognac** to each serving. (For more flavor and spike, use 1 tablespoon.) Flambé, if desired (see tips, pgs 38–39).

grand marnier winter warmer

Add **1 1/2 teaspoons Grand Marnier** to each serving. (For more flavor and spike, use 1 tablespoon.) Garnish with an **orange peel** and **whipped cream**, if desired.

ladies' night *crème de café*

Cool the coffee. Add **3 tablespoons coffee cream liqueur** to each serving. Serve in small cups.

rum and coffee night

Whip **1/2 cup heavy cream**. Add **1 tablespoons dark aged rum** to each serving. Top each with one third of the whipped cream. Garnish with a **small chocolate, dark or milk**.

vodka after-lunch coffee

Add **1 1/2 tablespoons vodka** to each serving.

157

hot
and
cold
drinks

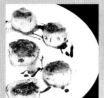

savory main dishes

In this chapter, I show you a new way to serve coffee at lunch and dinner: as an ingredient in the main course! When added to fruit sauces like blueberry, blackberry, or passion fruit, coffee creates beautiful hues and new tastes in savory dishes. And the combination of fruit, nuts, and coffee with poultry, grouper, or tuna is extraordinary. Serve the cornish game hens with blackberry-coffee sauce coupled with couscous or wild rice, and it will make a memorable meal.

filet mignon with coffee-blueberry sauce

4 bacon strips, about 2 ounces total
4 5- to 6-ounce slices beef filet, 1 1/2-inch thick
1/2 cup blueberries
1 tablespoon honey
1 teaspoon Worcestershire sauce
1 teaspoon freeze-dried or granulated instant coffee
1 teaspoon cornstarch
1/2 cup beef stock or broth (divided use)
1 teaspoon salt (divided use)
1/4 teaspoon freshly ground black pepper (divided use)
1 tablespoon olive oil

Toothpicks

1. Place the bacon strips on paper towels and microwave on high for 2 minutes to remove some of the fat. Let cool. Wrap each filet with a bacon strip and secure with a toothpick. Set aside.

2. Pureé the blueberries, honey, Worcestershire sauce, coffee, cornstarch, 1/4 cup of the stock, 1/2 teaspoon of the salt, and 1/8 teaspoon of the pepper in a blender until smooth. Pass through a sieve into a bowl and set aside.

3. Season the filets with the remaining salt and pepper. Heat the olive oil in a sauté pan over medium-high heat. When hot, add the filets.

4. Cook for 3 to 4 minutes on each side for medium rare. Remove from pan and set aside, covered, for 5 minutes.

5. Pour the remaining stock into the pan and cook with the pan juices for 2 to 3 minutes. Add the strained sauce and cook for 2 minutes more.

6. Serve the wrapped filets drizzled with the sauce.

Bacon-wrapped filets are a beautiful dish to serve company. The dark oak color and woodsy flavor of the sauce is amazing. You can cut the filet into bite-size pieces for cocktail parties, but make more sauce to go around.

flank steak

with wine-balsamic glaze

1 2-pound flank steak
1 tablespoon fresh thyme leaves
1/4 teaspoon freshly ground black pepper
3 teaspoons freeze-dried or granulated instant coffee (divided use)
1 tablespoon olive oil
1/2 teaspoon salt
3/4 cup beef stock or broth
1/4 cup red wine
1/4 cup balsamic vinegar
1/3 cup dark brown sugar
2 teaspoons all-purpose flour
2 teaspoons butter, softened

1. Rub the steak with the thyme, pepper, and 1 teaspoon of the coffee. Coat with the olive oil and refrigerate in a plastic zipper bag for 1 to 2 hours, or overnight.

2. When ready to cook, remove from refrigerator and bring to room temperature, about 10 minutes.

3. Heat a sauté pan over medium heat. Sprinkle the steak with salt and sear for 3 to 4 minutes on each side. Cover and cook for 5 minutes more. Remove from pan and set aside, covered, for 10 minutes.

4. Combine the stock, wine, vinegar, sugar, and remaining 2 teaspoons of coffee in a bowl. Pour into the pan and bring to a boil.

5. Make a paste by combining the flour and butter. Add to the pan and mix well. Cook 5 to 6 minutes, until sauce is slightly thickened and you can no longer taste the flour.

6. Cut the steak across the grain into thin slices. Serve with the warm sauce.

TIP: You can use this sauce instead of a demi-glace in other recipes.

Flank is a delicious cut of beef when cooked medium or medium rare. The sauce here is dark, shiny, and delicious—with a definite coffee taste that blends superbly with the wine-balsamic mixture. Depending on how salty your stock is, you can add more salt, if desired. You can even prepare this dish with chicken or vegetable stock. The leftover meat keeps refrigerated for a month and is great for wraps, fajitas, and sandwiches.

rib eyes with blackberry bbq sauce

This savory yet lightly sweet sauce—a wonderful change from traditional BBQ sauce—and the easy-to-cook cut of beef are perfect for lunch or an evening dinner outdoors.

4 boneless rib eye steaks, 1-inch thick (about 3 pounds total)
1/2 teaspoon freshly ground black pepper (divided use)
1 tablespoon olive oil
1 teaspoon salt (divided use)
1 cup blackberries
1/2 cup beef stock or broth
1/2 cup firmly packed dark brown sugar
1 tablespoon raspberry or red wine vinegar
1 tablespoon oyster sauce
2 1/2 teaspoons freeze-dried or granulated instant coffee
1 tablespoon demi-glace, optional
1 tablespoon cilantro, minced

Grill (optional)

1. Sprinkle steaks with 1/4 teaspoon of the pepper and rub with the olive oil. Heat a grill to medium high, or place a skillet over medium-high heat.

2. Sprinkle steaks with 1/2 teaspoon of the salt and cook for 5 to 6 minutes on each side for medium rare. Remove steaks from the grill or pan and set aside, covered, for 5 minutes.

3. Pureé the berries, stock, sugar, vinegar, oyster sauce, coffee, and the remaining salt and pepper in a blender until smooth. Pour through a sieve into a saucepan and cook for 5 to 7 minutes, or until thickened.

4. If using a grill, stir the demi-glace and cilantro into the sauce and serve warm with the steaks.

5. If using a skillet, add the sauce to the skillet and cook with the pan juices for 1 to 2 minutes, stir in the cilantro, and serve warm with the steaks.

163

savory
main
dishes

steak
stir-fry
with roasted
veggies

I use flour in this stir-fry to allow the beef to brown evenly despite the quick cooking time. It also thickens the sauce slightly, and allows the flavors from the broth and vegetables to blend deliciously.

Double recipe roasted vegetables with white balsamic dressing (pg 197)
1 1/2 pounds top sirloin or flank steak
2 garlic cloves, minced
1 tablespoon cilantro, minced
1/8 teaspoon freshly ground black pepper
2 tablespoons olive oil (divided use)
1 to 2 tablespoons all-purpose flour
1/2 teaspoon salt
3 (1 recipe) tablespoons balsamic reduction sauce (pg 32)
1/4 cup beef stock or broth

1. Prepare a double recipe of the roasted vegetables and set aside.

2. Partially freeze the meat; it will be easier to cut. Slice the meat into thin strips. Combine the steak strips with the garlic, cilantro, pepper, and 1 tablespoon of the olive oil and set aside in the refrigerator for 10 to 15 minutes.

3. Remove from refrigerator and dry with paper towels. Lightly coat the strips with the flour and salt. Place a large, heavy skillet over high heat. When hot, add the remaining olive oil, lower the heat to medium high, and add the steak strips. Cook for 2 to 3 minutes, keeping the pieces separated. (They will not brown evenly if they are too close. Work in batches, if necessary.)

4. Mix the balsamic reduction sauce and beef stock. Add to the skillet with the steak strips and cook until sauce thickens, about 2 minutes. Add the vegetables, and serve.

lamb chops
with sherry-mint sauce

Sherry-mint sauce goes so well with the coffee and lamb. The coffee softens the tangy mixture to a finger-licking goodness. I like to make this with tiny lamb chop racks, and can eat a whole one by myself. Whichever size you choose, buy the best-quality young lamb you can find. Try the recipe with white wine and chicken breast for a great variation.

8 5-ounce rib lamb chops, 1-inch thick (have your butcher french the bones)
3 tablespoons onion, grated
1 teaspoon garlic, minced
2 tablespoons fresh mint leaves, minced (divided use)
1/2 teaspoon freshly ground black pepper (divided use)
1 1/2 tablespoons olive oil (divided use)
1 1/2 teaspoons freeze-dried or granulated instant coffee
1 1/2 teaspoons water
3 tablespoons amontillado sherry
1 tablespoon sherry vinegar
1 1/2 tablespoons honey
1/2 cup beef stock or broth (divided use)
1/2 teaspoon salt (divided use)
1 tablespoon all-purpose flour
1 tablespoon butter, softened

1. Coat the chops with the onion, garlic, 1 tablespoon of the mint, 1/4 teaspoon of the pepper, and 1 tablespoon of the olive oil. Set aside in the refrigerator for 10 minutes.

2. In a medium bowl, dissolve the coffee in the water. Add the sherry, vinegar, honey, 1/4 cup of the stock, 1/4 teaspoon of the salt, and the remaining mint and pepper. Mix well and set aside.

3. Heat a sauté pan over medium heat. Sprinkle the chops with the remaining salt and sear for 2 to 3 minutes on each side. Add the sauce, cover, reduce heat to low, and cook 5 minutes. Turn the heat off, remove the chops and set aside, covered, for 5 minutes.

4. Pour the remaining stock into the sauté pan and deglaze the pan. Make a paste by combining the flour and butter. Add to the pan and mix well. Cook 3 to 4 minutes, until sauce is slightly thickened and you can no longer taste the flour. Serve warm with the chops.

VARIATIONS: For a rack of 8 to 9 baby lamb chops, sear in a sauté pan for 3 minutes on the meat side and 2 minutes on the bottom side. Transfer to a baking pan and bake for 20 minutes at 400°F for medium. Cut the rack into portions, and serve the sauce on top. You can also substitute 4 chicken breast halves for the lamb, white wine such as pinot grigio for the sherry, and white wine vinegar for the sherry vinegar.

pork tenderloins

with dijon mustard sauce

For everyday meals, pork tenderloins are the best! They are very practical—each one feeds two people and can be prepared in minutes. Then after a short rest, just slice them and arrange beautifully on a platter. Tenderloins are juicy and absorb marinades very well. If you have finicky children, as I do, serve one of the tenderloins without the sauce—it tastes great with just the seasoning. Leftover sauce can be used with Cornish hens or boneless chicken breasts.

4 SERVINGS

1 teaspoon freeze-dried or granulated instant coffee
2 teaspoons water
1/4 cup dark brown sugar
3 tablespoons heavy cream or half-and-half
2 tablespoons Dijon mustard
2 tablespoons onion, grated
2 garlic cloves, mashed
1 teaspoon fresh thyme leaves
1/2 teaspoon adobo seasoning (preferably Goya)
1/2 teaspoon salt
1/4 teaspoon freshly ground black pepper
2 1 1/4-pounds pork tenderloins
1/4 cup beef or chicken stock or broth

1. In a medium bowl, dissolve the coffee in the water. Add the sugar, cream or half-and-half, mustard, onion, garlic, thyme, adobo, salt, and pepper. Mix well to dissolve the sugar.

2. Place the tenderloins in a shallow dish, add the sauce, cover, and allow to marinate in the refrigerator for 20 to 30 minutes, or overnight.

3. When ready to cook, preheat the oven to 450°F. Remove the tenderloins and place on a rack over a baking pan.

4. Mix the stock into the sauce and pour into the baking pan. Bake until a thermometer inserted into a tenderloin reads 160°F, or a clear liquid comes out of the meat when you prick it, about 25 to 30 minutes.

5. Remove the tenderloins from the pan and cover with foil for 5 minutes. Stir pan juices and sauce with a spatula. Slice the tenderloin into pieces about 1- to 1 1/4-inch thick. Pour the sauce over the slices, or serve it on the side.

167

pork tenderloins

with port wine sauce

I really like to cook meats with port wine, and I often use Cinzano Rosso in my pork recipes. I have done so for years with my pork stuffing for turkey, and the flavors are distinct and wonderful. This sauce is somewhat spicy and sweet; the basil and coffee complement each other well.

4 SERVINGS

1 teaspoon freeze-dried or granulated instant coffee
5 teaspoons water (divided use)
1/2 ruby port wine or Cinzano Rosso (sweet red vermouth)
1/4 cup dark brown sugar
2 garlic cloves, minced
1 tablespoon basil, julienned (about 10 leaves)
1/2 teaspoon salt
1/4 teaspoon aniseed, toasted*
1/4 teaspoon cumin seeds, toasted*
1/4 teaspoon freshly ground black pepper
2 1 1/4-pounds pork tenderloins
1/4 cup beef or chicken broth
1 teaspoon cornstarch

1. In a medium bowl, dissolve the coffee in 2 teaspoons of the water. Add the port wine or vermouth, sugar, garlic, basil, salt, aniseed, cumin, and pepper. Mix well to dissolve the sugar.

2. Place the tenderloins in a shallow dish, add the sauce, cover, and allow to marinate in the refrigerator for 20 to 30 minutes, or overnight.

3. When ready to cook, preheat the oven to 450°F. Remove the tenderloins and place on a rack over a baking pan.

4. Mix the stock into the sauce and pour into the baking pan. Bake until a thermometer inserted into a tenderloin reads 160°F, or a clear liquid comes out of the meat when you prick it, about 25 to 30 minutes.

5. Remove the tenderloins from the pan and cover with foil for 5 minutes. Stir pan juices and sauce with a spatula. Mix the cornstarch with the remaining water and stir into the sauce. Transfer to a saucepan and cook over medium-high heat for 2 to 3 minutes, or until slightly thickened.

6. Slice the tenderloin into pieces about 1- to 1 1/4-inch thick. Pour the sauce over the slices, or serve it on the side.

*See tips, pgs 38–39

pork chops
with sesame
sauce

One-inch-thick chops are perfect for this recipe—thinner chops can dry out and thicker ones tend to undercook. Port wine is great for making sauces when you cannot get your hands on a good demi-glace.

4 pork chops, 1-inch thick (about 1 1/2 pounds total)
3 tablespoons onion, grated
2 cloves garlic, mashed
1 1/2 tablespoons cilantro, minced
1 tablespoon olive oil
1 teaspoon freeze-dried or granulated instant coffee
2 teaspoons water
1/4 cup port wine
1/4 cup maple syrup
4 teaspoons rice vinegar
1/8 teaspoon sesame oil
1/2 teaspoon salt (divided use)
1/4 teaspoon freshly ground black pepper (divide use)
1 tablespoon sesame seeds

1. Preheat the oven to 400°F. Coat the chops with the onion, garlic, cilantro, and olive oil. Set aside in the refrigerator for 10 minutes.

2. In a medium bowl, dissolve the coffee in the water. Add the port wine, syrup, vinegar, oil, 1/4 teaspoon of the salt, and 1/8 teaspoon of the pepper. Mix well and set aside.

3. Heat a large heavy skillet over medium heat. Sprinkle the chops with the sesame seeds and the remaining salt and pepper, and sear for 3 minutes on each side. Transfer the skillet to the oven and cook for 10 minutes, or until a thermometer inserted into a chop reads 160°F.

4. Remove the chops from the skillet and set aside, covered. Add the sauce to the skillet and cook over medium-low heat for 3 to 5 minutes. Pour the sauce over the chops, or serve on the side.

169

cornish game hens with blackberry-coffee sauce

2 1 1/4-pound Cornish game hens
1/3 cup dried Zante currants
2 teaspoons garlic, minced
3 tablespoons olive oil (divided use)
4 sprigs rosemary (divided use)
1 teaspoon salt (divided use)
1/4 teaspoon freshly ground black pepper (divided use)
3/4 cup chicken stock (divided use)
1 cup blackberries
1/2 cup red wine
5 tablespoons sugar
1 tablespoon Dijon mustard
1 tablespoon freeze-dried or granulated instant coffee

Kitchen twine

1. Preheat the oven to 425°F. Rinse the hens with water and pat dry. Place the hens on a rack over a baking pan.

2. Combine the currants, garlic, 2 tablespoons of the olive oil, the leaves from 2 sprigs of rosemary, 3/4 teaspoon of the salt, and 1/8 teaspoon of the pepper. Place a little less than half of the mixture into the cavity of each hen and rub the rest on the outside. Don't worry if the currants fall off the hens onto the baking pan. Tie the legs with twine and place 1 sprig of rosemary over each hen.

3. Add 1/2 cup of the chicken stock to the pan, and bake for 45 to 50 minutes. Remove the hens from the rack and set aside, covered, for 5 minutes.

4. Purée the blackberries, wine, sugar, mustard, coffee, and the remaining chicken stock, salt, and pepper in a blender until smooth. Pour through a sieve into the baking pan, scrape up any bits, transfer to a saucepan over medium heat, and cook for 1 to 2 minutes.

5. Remove the rosemary sprigs and twine from the hens. Cut the hens in half and serve with the sauce.

Cornish hens are beautiful, super simple to prepare, and full of taste. Some people eat a whole one, but for me half is plenty. The woodsy, full-bodied sauce is also great with pork and seafood.

170

coffee curried
chicken

This delicious recipe tastes best when prepared with chicken with bones. They make the chicken more flavorful and juicier, even if slightly overcooked. The sauce is delicate and somewhat sweet. It can also be drizzled over white rice and topped with shredded cheese and toasted coconut for a great side dish.

2 SERVINGS

1 teaspoon freeze-dried or granulated instant coffee
2 teaspoons water
2/3 cup plain yogurt
3 tablespoons honey
1 teaspoon garlic, minced
1 teaspoon cornstarch
1 teaspoon curry powder
1/2 teaspoon salt
1/4 teaspoon freshly ground black pepper
2 chicken breast halves, with bones and skin (about 1 1/2 pounds total)
2 tablespoons raisins
2 tablespoons cognac
3 tablespoons slivered almonds, toasted*
2 tablespoons coconut, toasted*

1. In a medium bowl, dissolve the coffee in the water. Add the yogurt, honey, garlic, cornstarch, curry, salt, and pepper. Mix well.

2. Place the chicken in a shallow dish, add the sauce, cover, and allow to marinate in the refrigerator for 1 to 2 hours, or overnight.

3. When ready to cook, preheat the oven to 400°F. Remove the chicken from the refrigerator and bring to room temperature, about 10 minutes.

4. Place the chicken in a baking pan, and add the sauce. Bake for 40 to 45 minutes, or until a thermometer inserted into the chicken reads 160°F. Remove chicken from the pan and set aside, covered.

5. Heat the raisins and cognac in a small saucepan over medium heat until the raisins plump up, about 2 minutes, and then flambé.* Remove from heat and set aside, covered.

6. Add the raisins and almonds to the sauce in the baking pan, mix, and spoon over the breasts to serve. Sprinkle with the toasted coconut.

VARIATION: This recipe can also be prepared with half-and-half, but I use yogurt because it is lighter, easier to digest, has a consistency that is easier to work with, and carries the flavors through the sauce better.

*See tips, pgs 38–39

chicken with dried apricots and pine nuts

A beautiful presentation in just minutes. Apricots and pine nuts bring color and flavor, contrast nicely with the coffee, and highlight the chicken. Slice the rolled chicken on the bias with an electric knife for a quick, perfect cut. Serve with just a drizzle of sauce on top and the rest on the side.

2 SERVINGS; 2/3 CUP SAUCE

2 skinless, boneless chicken breasts (about 1 1/4 to 1 1/2pounds total)
1/2 teaspoon salt (divided use)
1/4 teaspoon freshly ground black pepper (divided use)
1 tablespoon olive oil (divided use)
3 tablespoons scallion, minced (white part only)
1 teaspoon minced garlic
2 tablespoons basil, julienned (about 20 leaves)* (divided use)
1 1/2 teaspoons freeze-dried or granulated instant coffee (divided use)
4 dried apricots, thinly sliced (divided use)
4 tablespoons pine nuts, toasted* (divided use)
1 1/2 teaspoons water
1/2 cup plain yogurt
2 tablespoons chicken stock or broth
1 tablespoon honey
1 teaspoon cornstarch

Toothpicks

1. Preheat the oven to 400°F. Pound each chicken breast to 1/4-inch thickness and season with 1/4 teaspoon of the salt and 1/8 teaspoon of the pepper. Drizzle with 1 1/2 teaspoons of the olive oil and set aside.

2. In a small sauté pan, combine the scallion, garlic, 1 tablespoon of the basil, 1/2 teaspoon of the coffee, and the remaining oil, salt, and pepper. Cook for 2 to 3 minutes over low heat, until fragrant. Reserve 1 tablespoon each of the apricots and pine nuts, and stir the rest into the mixture. Transfer to a plate and set aside to cool.

3. In a small bowl, dissolve the remaining coffee in the water. Add the yogurt, stock, honey, and cornstarch. Pour into the sauté pan, place back on the heat, and bring to a boil. Add the re-served apricots and pine nuts and the remaining basil. Cook for 1 to 2 minutes, just until thickened. Keep warm.

4. Spread half of the cooled apricot–pine nut mixture over each chicken breast, roll, and secure with wooden toothpicks. Place a griddle or heavy sauté pan over medium heat. When hot, remove from heat and spray with nonstick cooking oil. Return the pan to heat, add the rolled chicken, and cook for 2 to 3 minutes, turning to sear and brown on all sides.

5. Transfer the rolled chicken to a shallow baking pan and bake for 15 to 20 minutes. Remove the rolled chicken from the pan, add any pan juices to the sauce, and reheat. Slice each roll into pieces and serve with the warm sauce.

VARIATION: This recipe can also be prepared with half-and-half. If using half-and-half, do not add the cornstarch in step 5.

*See tips, pgs 38–39

chicken strips

I based this recipe on my sister Sylvia's chicken strips. It is very easy to prepare and could feed an army if you adjust the quantities. Prepare the chicken ahead of time, and you can quickly cook a last-minute meal.

1 1/2 pounds skinless, boneless chicken breasts
1 teaspoon freeze-dried or granulated instant coffee
2 teaspoons water
1/2 cup honey
1/4 cup Dijon mustard
2/3 cup plain, whole milk yogurt
1 teaspoon cornstarch
1/2 cup unsalted peanuts, chopped
1/4 cup fresh bread crumbs or panko
1/2 teaspoon salt
1/4 teaspoon freshly ground black pepper

1. Cut the chicken breasts into long strips across the grain. Place in a shallow bowl or dish.

2. In a bowl, dissolve the coffee in the water. Add the honey, mustard, yogurt, and cornstarch. Mix well and pour over the chicken strips. Refrigerate for 10 to 15 minutes, or longer, if desired.

3. When ready to cook, preheat the oven to 450°F. Remove the strips from the refrigerator and bring to room temperature, about 10 minutes.

4. Mix the peanuts, bread crumbs, salt, and pepper in a bowl.

5. Lightly spray a shallow baking pan with nonstick cooking oil. Coat the strips with the crumb mixture, and place in the pan.

6. Bake for 20 to 25 minutes, or until a thermometer inserted into the strips reads 160°F. Serve warm.

tamarind-spiced chicken breasts

Exotic, sensuous, somewhat spicy, and crunchy—this is what I call an aphrodisiac recipe. Tart, yet sweet and savory, like the breeze of the tropical islands. Try it for Valentine's Day or on a special occasion.

1 1/2 teaspoon freeze-dried or granulated instant coffee
1/2 cup chicken stock
1/4 cup firmly-packed dark brown sugar
2 tablespoons tamarind paste (see tips, pgs 38–39)
2 tablespoons scallion, sliced (green and white)
1 teaspoon garlic, minced
1 teaspoon cornstarch
1/4 teaspoon ground cumin
1/4 teaspoon freshly ground black pepper
2 1/2 tablespoons cilantro, minced (divided use)
1 teaspoon salt (divided use)
2 boneless chicken breast halves, with skin (about 1 1/4 to 1 1/2 pounds total)
2 tablespoons chopped unsalted cashews, optional

1. In a heavy saucepan, dissolve the coffee in the chicken stock. Stir in the sugar, tamarind paste, scallion, garlic, cornstarch, cumin, pepper, 2 tablespoons of the cilantro, and 1/2 teaspoon of the salt. Bring to a boil and cook about 1 minute. Remove from heat and set aside to cool.

2. Place the chicken breasts in a shallow dish, add the cooled sauce, cover, and allow to marinate in the refrigerator for 1 to 2 hours, or overnight.

3. When ready to cook, preheat the oven to 400°F. Remove the chicken breasts from the refrigerator and bring to room temperature, about 10 minutes.

4. Sprinkle the chicken with the remaining cilantro and cashews, if using.

5. Bake for 40 to 45 minutes, or until until a thermometer inserted into a chicken breast reads 160°F.

6. Stir the sauce in the baking dish, and serve over the chicken breasts.

tuna with yellow pepper chutney

Tuna is one of my favorite fish, and I usually eat it rare. You can cook it to medium rare, if desired, and enjoy the beautiful texture and color. This dish is a "food for all of your senses."

2 SERVINGS

2 tablespoons maple syrup
1 tablespoon balsamic reduction sauce (pg 32)
1 tablespoon grainy Dijon mustard
1/2 teaspoon salt
1/4 teaspoon freshly ground black pepper
2 6-ounce tuna filets, 1-inch thick
1 tablespoon olive oil
1 cup (1/2 recipe) yellow pepper chutney (pg 187)

1. Mix the maple syrup, balsamic sauce, mustard, salt, and pepper in a bowl. Rub over the tuna steaks and set aside for 15 minutes.

2. Place a heavy sauté pan over medium-high heat. When hot, coat with the oil. Cook the steaks for 1 to 1 1/2 minutes on each side for rare.

3. Transfer the tuna to serving plates. Heat the chutney in the sauté pan, and serve with the steaks.

grouper with almonds

and white wine

Toasted almonds and white wine go great with fish. Prepare the sauce ahead of time and then just bake, serve, and enjoy.

1 tablespoon oil
3 tablespoons onion, minced
2 tablespoon cilantro, minced
1 garlic clove, minced
3/4 teaspoon salt
1/2 teaspoon freshly ground black pepper
2 teaspoons freeze-dried or granulated instant coffee
2 teaspoons water
1/2 cup plain yogurt
1/4 cup fish stock
1 tablespoon honey
2 tablespoons white wine
1 1/2 teaspoons cornstarch
2 6-ounce grouper filets*
3 tablespoons slivered almonds, toasted (see tips, pgs 38–39)

1. Preheat the oven to 425°F.

2. In a sauté pan, cook the oil, onion, cilantro, garlic, salt, and pepper over low heat for 2 to 3 minutes, or until fragrant.

3. In a medium bowl, dissolve the coffee in the water. Add the yogurt, stock, honey, white wine, and cornstarch. Mix well, add to the sauté pan, and bring to a boil. Cook for 1 to 2 minutes, and set aside to cool.

4. Place the fish in a small baking pan and cover with the sauce. Bake for 10 to 12 minutes.

5. Transfer the fish to serving plates, pour the sauce over the top, sprinkle with the almonds, and serve.

*Any white, firm-fleshed fish will work in this recipe.

177

savory
main
dishes

scallops with savory yellow gooseberry sauce

Another exotic and delicious recipe that you can prepare in no time! The fresh, light, and summery sauce can be used with most seafood. Or, try this sauce with green beans—you will be surprised at the great taste.

2 SERVINGS; SCANT 2/3 CUP SAUCE

SAVORY YELLOW GOOSEBERRY SAUCE
1/2 cup yellow gooseberries*
2 tablespoons white wine
2 tablespoons fish stock
2 tablespoons honey
1 3/4 teaspoons freeze-dried or granulated instant coffee
1/2 teaspoon salt
1/8 teaspoon freshly ground black pepper
1 1/2 teaspoons all-purpose flour
1 1/2 teaspoons butter, softened
1 tablespoon basil, julienned (about 10 leaves)*

1 tablespoon olive oil
12 large scallops, thawed if frozen (patted dry)
1/2 teaspoon salt
1/4 teaspoon freshly ground black pepper
1 tablespoon warm balsamic reduction sauce (pg 32)

1. To prepare the savory yellow gooseberry sauce, purée the gooseberries, wine, stock, honey, coffee, salt, and pepper in a blender until smooth, about 15 seconds. Transfer to a small saucepan.

2. Make a paste by combining the flour and butter. Add to the pan and mix well. Simmer for 3 minutes, until sauce is slightly thickened and you can no longer taste the flour. Add the basil, cook 1 minute more, and remove from the heat.

3. Heat the oil in a skillet or sauté pan over medium-high heat and add the scallops. Sprinkle with salt and pepper and sear for 2 minutes on each side. Add the gooseberry sauce and cook for 2 minutes more.

4. Divide the sauce onto 2 serving plates, arrange the scallops, and serve drizzled with a bit of balsamic reduction sauce.

*See tips, pgs 38–39

balsamic salmon

and portobellos

Delicious, fresh, and colorful—this dish is like a ray of sunlight. Salmon goes perfectly with balsamic vinegar and coffee … and so do portobellos! The secret to this recipe is browning the salmon in a hot oven and allowing the portobellos to absorb the sauce.

2 6-ounce or 1 12-ounce salmon filet
1 large or 2 medium portobello mushrooms
1 teaspoon salt (divided use)
3/8 teaspoon freshly ground black pepper (divided use)
1/2 cup orange juice
2 tablespoons balsamic vinegar
2 tablespoons fish stock
3 tablespoons honey
1 1/2 teaspoons Dijon mustard
1 tablespoon basil, julienned (about 10 leaves)*
2 teaspoons freeze-dried or granulated instant coffee

1. Cut the fish into 2-inch pieces and the portobellos into 1/8-inch slices. Place in a shallow nonreactive* bowl and sprinkle with 1/2 teaspoon of the salt and 1/4 teaspoon of the pepper.

2. In a bowl, combine the juice, vinegar, stock, honey, mustard, basil, coffee, and the remaining salt and pepper. Mix until the honey is well dissolved, pour over the fish and mushrooms, and refrigerate for 15 to 30 minutes.

3. When ready to cook, preheat the oven to 450°F. Remove from the refrigerator and transfer to a baking pan.

4. Bake for 10 to 12 minutes for medium. Divide the fish and mushrooms onto 2 serving plates, top with sauce from the pan, and serve.

*See tips, pgs 38–39

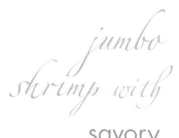

jumbo shrimp with

savory passion fruit sauce

This delicate dish is great for a dinner with guests or a relaxed, romantic evening. I have served this recipe with a combination of seafood and it works out beautifully. Try it with lobster tails and scallops for a fantastic presentation.

2 SERVINGS; 3/4 CUP SAUCE

1 pound (about 10) jumbo shrimp, peeled and deveined
1/2 teaspoon Old Bay seasoning
1/2 teaspoon salt
1/4 teaspoon freshly ground black pepper
2 tablespoons olive oil (divided use)

SAVORY PASSION FRUIT SAUCE
9 tablespoons passion fruit pulp*
9 tablespoons fish stock
3 tablespoons light brown sugar
1 1/2 teaspoons cornstarch
1 1/2 teaspoons coffee
1/2 teaspoon salt
1/4 teaspoon freshly ground black pepper
1 tablespoon cold butter cut in small cubes

2 tablespoons warm caramel coffee sauce (pg 33)

1. Combine the shrimp with the seasoning, salt, pepper, and 1 tablespoon of the oil in a plastic zipper bag. Refrigerate for 10 minutes or until ready to use.

2. To prepare the savory passion fruit sauce, pureé the passion fruit pulp, stock, sugar, cornstarch, coffee, salt and pepper in a blender until smooth, about 15 seconds.

3. Transfer to a nonreactive*, heavy saucepan and bring to a boil over high heat. Cook for 3 minutes, or until the sauce thickens slightly. Remove from heat, add the butter, and mix.

4. Place the remaining oil in a hot skillet or a sauté pan over medium-high heat. Add the shrimp, keeping them separated, and cook for 2 to 3 minutes on each side.

5. Divide the sauce between two serving plates, arrange the shrimp, and serve drizzled with a bit of caramel coffee sauce.

*See tips, pgs 38–39

spiced tuna with

mandarin-coffee sauce

This rub is also great with pork ribs. Serve the tuna steaks cut in half or quarters to showcase the fantastic deep red color of the fish.

SPICE RUB
1 tablespoon cilantro, minced
1 teaspoon fresh thyme leaves
1 teaspoon ground coriander
1 tablespoon dark brown sugar
1 teaspoon salt
1/4 teaspoon freshly ground black pepper

2 6-ounce tuna steaks (1-inch thick)
1 tablespoon olive oil

MANDARIN-COFFEE SAUCE
2 teaspoons freeze-dried or granulated instant coffee
1/2 cup mandarin or tangerine juice
2 tablespoons honey
2 teaspoons soy sauce
1/4 teaspoon salt
1/4 teaspoon dark sesame oil
1/8 teaspoon freshly ground black pepper
1 tablespoon all-purpose flour
1 tablespoon butter, softened
1/4 teaspoon fresh ginger, minced

1. To prepare the spice rub, grind the cilantro, thyme, and coriander to a paste with a mortar and pestle or spice grinder. Transfer to a small bowl, and add the sugar, salt, and pepper.

2. Place the tuna steaks on a plate, coat with the spice rub, and set aside for 15 minutes.

3. To prepare the mandarin-coffee sauce, dissolve the coffee in the mandarin juice in a saucepan. Add the honey, soy sauce, salt, sesame oil, and pepper. Make a paste by combining the flour and butter. Add to the pan and mix well. Cook over medium heat for 5 to 7 minutes, or until sauce is slightly thickened and you can no longer taste the flour. Add the ginger, remove from heat, and set aside.

4. Place the olive oil in a heavy sauté pan over medium-high heat, and cook the tuna steaks for 1 to 1 1/2 minutes on each side for rare.

5. Transfer the steaks to serving plates. Reheat the sauce in the sauté pan, and serve poured around the tuna.

181

savory
main
dishes

greens and more

Who says coffee and vegetables don't go well together? Surely you won't after trying these unique recipes. You can serve many of these salads on their own as a light meal—or make an elegant dinner by pairing them with a recipe from the savory main dishes chapter. Choose the pasta made with chevre, tomatoes, and herbs, or the mango and prosciutto salad made with coffee syrup and basil. Dress up everyday greens with one of the sophisticated coffee-infused vinaigrettes.

salad dressings **and condiments**

The dressings here work well with many different dishes—not just salads. Try them on seafood, poultry, and vegetables. When working with vinaigrettes, use a nonreactive bowl (see tips, pgs 38–39).

asian vinaigrette

2/3 CUP, 4 SERVINGS

My favorite of all! Keep this dressing on hand at home or the office. Mix with some greens and vegetables and voilà—a midday energy boost!

2 tablespoons parsley, minced
4 teaspoons rice vinegar
4 teaspoons maple syrup
1 teaspoon freeze-dried or granulated instant coffee
3/4 teaspoon salt
1/4 teaspoon freshly ground black pepper
1/4 teaspoon dark sesame oil
6 tablespoons canola oil

In a nonreactive bowl, mix the parsley, vinegar, syrup, coffee, salt, and pepper. Add the oils and whisk with a fork until thick and emulsified.

basil-balsamic vinaigrette

1/3 CUP, 2 TO 3 SERVINGS

A very versatile dressing—try it on vegetables like green beans and asparagus, or even sliced tomatoes.

4 teaspoons balsamic vinegar (preferably Roland)
1 tablespoon honey
2 teaspoons fresh basil, minced
1 teaspoon freeze-dried or granulated instant coffee
1/2 teaspoon salt
1/4 teaspoon freshly ground black pepper
1/4 cup canola oil

In a nonreactive bowl, mix the vinegar, honey, basil, coffee, salt, and pepper until the honey has dissolved. Add the oil and whisk with a fork until thick and emulsified.

creamy low-sugar red wine vinaigrette
1/3 CUP, 2 SERVINGS

This creamy dressing can be used as a dip for hearts of palm or mushrooms, and will liven up basic raw veggies like carrots and celery.

1 1/2 tablespoons plain yogurt
2 teaspoons red wine vinegar
1 packet artificial sweetener (I use Splenda)
1/2 teaspoon freeze-dried or granulated instant coffee
1/4 teaspoon Dijon mustard
1/2 teaspoon salt
1/8 teaspoon freshly ground black pepper
2 1/2 tablespoons canola oil

In a nonreactive bowl, mix the yogurt, vinegar, sweetener, coffee, mustard, salt, and pepper. Add the oil and whisk with a fork until thick and emulsified.

creamy yogurt dressing
3/4 CUP, 4 TO 6 SERVINGS

This simple dressing can be kept refrigerated for more than a week if you add the cilantro just before each use. Try other herbs if you like, such as mint, dill, or basil. Serve it over lettuce, cooked vegetables, baked or boiled potatoes, rice, poultry, or even fruit.

2 tablespoons chopped cilantro
1 tablespoon honey
3/4 teaspoon savory coffee syrup (pg 37)
1/2 teaspoon salt
1/4 teaspoon freshly ground black pepper
3/4 cup plain nonfat yogurt

In a bowl, mix cilantro, honey, coffee syrup, salt, and pepper until the honey has dissolved. Add the yogurt and mix. If you only partially blend, you will create a swirl design.

sherry vinaigrette
1/3 CUP, 2 SERVINGS

A complex group of ingredients takes this vinaigrette to another level. Serve it with your nicest meals.

2 teaspoons honey
2 teaspoons sherry vinegar
1 teaspoon rosemary leaves, chopped (1 sprig)
1/2 teaspoon freeze-dried or granulated instant coffee
1/4 teaspoon salt
1/8 teaspoon freshly ground black pepper
2 tablespoons canola oil

In a nonreactive bowl, mix the honey, vinegar, rosemary, coffee, salt, and pepper until the honey has dissolved. Add the oil and whisk with a fork until thick and emulsified.

white balsamic vinaigrette
1/4 CUP, 2 SERVINGS

A twist on regular balsamic—very interesting. It has good acidity, yet it's soft and almost colorless for when you want to highlight a food's color, such as berries and hearts of palm.

2 teaspoons white balsamic vinegar
1 teaspoon firmly packed light brown sugar
1 teaspoon fresh cilantro or thyme, minced
1/2 teaspoon freeze-dried or granulated instant coffee
1/4 teaspoon salt
1/8 teaspoon freshly ground black pepper
2 1/2 tablespoons olive oil

In a nonreactive bowl, mix the vinegar, sugar, cilantro or thyme, coffee, salt, and pepper until the sugar has dissolved. Add the oil and whisk with a fork until thick and emulsified.

passion
for
coffee

white wine vinaigrette

A traditional dressing for a beginner cook. It's just perfect.

1 1/2 teaspoons honey
2 teaspoons white wine vinegar
1/2 teaspoon freeze-dried or granulated instant coffee
1/2 teaspoon salt
1/8 teaspoon freshly ground black pepper
2 tablespoons olive oil

In a nonreactive bowl, mix the honey, vinegar, coffee, salt, and pepper until the honey has dissolved. Add the oil and whisk with a fork until thick and emulsified.

yellow pepper chutney
2 CUPS

This is another one of my favorite recipes. Sometimes I prepare it with all yellow peppers, sometimes all red, and other times I use three differently colored peppers! I just love playing around with the serving possibilities. I'll serve it over a warm Brie or Camembert cheese, with fish, or add it to a salad with blue or Roquefort cheese.

1 1/2 tablespoons olive oil
1/4 cup shallot, minced
2 teaspoons minced garlic
1 teaspoon coriander
1 teaspoon mustard seeds
1 teaspoon curry powder
1 teaspoon garam marsala
1/2 teaspoon salt
1/2 teaspoon pepper
3 1/2 cups yellow peppers, julienned (about 3 peppers)
1/3 cup granulated sugar
2 tablespoons rice vinegar
1 teaspoon hot pepper, minced, optional

Place the oil in a heavy saucepan over medium heat. Add the shallot, garlic, coriander, mustard seeds, curry, garam marsala, salt, and pepper. Cook for 3 to 5 minutes, or until the shallot is translucent and the mixture is very aromatic. Add the peppers, sugar, vinegar, and hot pepper, if desired. Reduce the heat to medium low and cook for 40 minutes, stirring occasionally. Cool and refrigerate until ready to use.

asparagus
with savory
coffee syrup

Serve asparagus with any meal.
It goes with everything and
makes any meal sophisticated.

1/2 pound fresh green asparagus (1/4-inch thick, or thinner)
1 teaspoon freeze-dried or granulated instant coffee
1 1/2 teaspoons butter
1 teaspoon shallot, minced
1 teaspoon parsley, minced
1/4 teaspoon granulated sugar
1/8 teaspoon salt
1/8 teaspoon freshly ground black pepper
2 tablespoons savory coffee syrup (pg 37)

1. Rinse and trim the blunt ends of the asparagus stalks. Place the asparagus and coffee in a wide sauté pan, and add water to almost cover. Add the butter, shallot, parsley, sugar, salt, and pepper.

2. Bring to a simmer and cook until the asparagus stalks feel somewhat tender, but are still firm when pricked. Remove from the pan and set aside on a rack.

3. Keep the pan over the heat and boil until almost all of the liquid has evaporated. When the pan is almost dry and starts to sizzle, add the coffee syrup and return the asparagus to the pan, to flavor and reheat them. Serve.

VARIATION: Try tying three-spear bunches together with julienned strips of roasted red pepper or scallions (using green parts that have been blanched in boiling salted water for 10 seconds).

4 SERVINGS

asian
cranberry
and almond
salad

The flavors of dried cranberries
and sesame bring out the coffee
and will liven up any meal.

2/3 cup (1 recipe) asian vinaigrette (pg 184)
1 tablespoon pickled ginger, julienned
3 tablespoons dried cranberries, chopped (divided use)
1/4 cup slivered almonds, toasted (see tips, pgs 38–39) (divided use)
2 heads red leaf lettuce, washed, dried, and torn
1 cooked chicken breast, optional

1. Prepare the vinaigrette. Add the ginger and half of the cranberries and almonds.

2. When ready to serve, strain over the lettuce. Sprinkle the remaining half of the cranberries and almonds over the salad.

3. To turn this into a full meal, cut the chicken breast in half. Thinly slice it on the bias and arrange over the salad.

189

greens
and
more

artichoke heart and pearl onion salad

Artichoke hearts and pearl onions love balsamic vinegar—they all blend well and highlight each other's flavors.

1/3 cup (1 recipe) basil-balsamic vinaigrette (pg 184)
1 6-ounce jar marinated artichoke hearts, drained
1 cup fresh pearl onions, or thawed frozen onions
1 tablespoon butter
1 tablespoon light brown sugar
2 tablespoons balsamic vinegar
1/4 teaspoon salt
1/8 teaspoon freshly ground black pepper
1 teaspoon savory coffee syrup (pg 37)
2 heads of curly, red lettuce

1. Prepare the vinaigrette. Drain the artichokes, cover with the vinaigrette, and set aside until ready to serve.

2. To prepare fresh pearl onions, bring a medium saucepan of water to a boil, add the onions, cook for 1 minute, drain, and peel. (Skip this step if using frozen onions.)

3. Sauté the onions and butter in a heavy saucepan over medium-low heat for 2 to 3 minutes. Add the sugar, vinegar, salt, and pepper, mix, and cook for 2 to 3 minutes more, or until lightly golden. Add the coffee syrup, mix, and remove from heat. Allow the onions to cool to room temperature.

4. Drain the vinaigrette from the artichokes into a small pitcher and cut the artichokes into quarters. Arrange the lettuce on a platter or individual serving plates.

5. Pour the vinaigrette over the lettuce, arrange the onions and artichokes on top, and serve.

hearts of palm
and pearl onion sauté

2 to 3 1-inch fresh hearts of palm
1/2 pound white or yellow pearl onions
1 tablespoon garlic, minced
1 green onion, minced
2 tablespoons cilantro, minced
2 tablespoons honey
1 tablespoon rice vinegar
1/2 tablespoon granulated sugar
3/4 teaspoon salt
1/4 teaspoon pepper
1 tablespoon oil
1 tablespoon butter
3 tablespoons (1 recipe) balsamic reduction sauce (pg 32)

1. Slice hearts of palm lengthwise into eighths. To prepare fresh pearl onions, bring a medium saucepan of water to a boil, add the onions, cook for 1 minute, drain, and peel.

2. In a nonreactive bowl, mix the garlic, green onion, cilantro, honey, vinegar, sugar, salt, and pepper until the honey has dissolved. Add the onions and palm slices, and mix with a fork until well coated. Set aside until ready to cook, or at least 1 hour.

3. Heat a sauté pan over medium heat and add the oil and butter. Pour the mixture into the pan and cook for 5 to 7 minutes, or until lightly browned. Add the balsamic reduction sauce and cook 1 minute more. Remove from the heat and serve.

mozzarella, tomato, and pasta salad

I usually prepare two or three vinaigrettes for the week and keep them refrigerated. This is a great way to help you make a quick and healthy meal when you're short on time. Take them to the office or on a road trip! And always use the best fresh mozzarella you can get.

mango and prosciutto salad

Oh, how very Mediterranean—I am transported to the rocks and sea when I prepare this salad. Great for eating outdoors in the summer. Use a mango that is not quite completely ripe—one that still has a little firmness.

1/3 cup (1 recipe) basil-balsamic vinaigrette (pg 184)
1 cup cherry tomatoes, halved
5 cups water
1 1/2 teaspoons salt
1 1/2 teaspoons cooking oil
1 1/2 cups penne pasta
4 ounces fresh mozzarella
4 basil leaves, julienned (see tips, pg 38–39)
1 1/2 teaspoons freshly ground black pepper

1. Prepare the vinaigrette. Add the tomatoes and set aside.

2. Bring the water to a boil in a saucepan over high heat. Add the salt, oil, and pasta and cook until al dente.

3. Drain the pasta, place in a bowl, add the vinaigrette and tomatoes, and allow to cool. Drain the mozzarella and cut into 1/2-inch cubes.

4. When the pasta has cooled, add the mozzarella, basil, and pepper. Toss gently and serve.

TIP: Place the tomatoes in the vinaigrette and refrigerate for 2 or 3 days. They will fully absorb the flavor, and you can serve them on their own!

2 SERVINGS

1/3 cup (1 recipe) sherry vinaigrette (pg 186)
1/2 cup thinly sliced mango
2 tablespoons basil, julienned (about 20 leaves) (see tips, pgs 38–39)
3 cups torn curly, red lettuce, washed and dried
4 ounces thinly sliced prosciutto
2 teaspoons savory coffee syrup (pg 37)

1. Prepare the vinaigrette, add the mango and basil, and set aside.

2. When ready to serve, place the lettuce on a platter or individual serving plates and arrange the prosciutto on top.

3. Add the vinaigrette with mango and basil, drizzle with savory coffee syrup, and serve.

193

greens
and
more

squid
salad with
caramelized
coffee pecans

This is the best seafood salad!
Prepare the squid quickly—cook
it for less than a minute to ensure
tender rings. The yogurt and
pecans make this a filling dish.
If you wish, you can substitute
basil or dill for the cilantro.

1 cup caramelized coffee pecans (pg 28)
3/4 cup (1 recipe) creamy yogurt dressing (pg 185)
6 ounces squid rings
1 teaspoon garlic, minced
1 teaspoon cilantro, minced
1/2 teaspoon salt
1/4 teaspoon freshly ground black pepper
1/2 tablespoon olive oil
1 tablespoon savory coffee syrup (pg 37)
4 cups mesclun greens

1. Prepare the caramelized coffee pecans and set aside. Prepare the dressing in a large bowl and set aside.

2. Combine the squid, garlic, cilantro, salt, and pepper in a bowl. Add the oil and mix. Set aside for 10 minutes.

3. Spray a sauté pan with nonstick cooking oil, add the squid, and sauté over medium heat for just under 1 minute. Remove immediately from the heat, add the coffee syrup to the pan, and then add the mixture to the vinaigrette. Let cool.

4. When ready to serve, add the mesclun to the bowl and gently toss with the dressing and squid.

5. Arrange on a platter or individual serving plates and serve sprinkled with the pecans.

parmesan—
grape salad

This salad can be a side dish for pork or other meats—it lightens up the menu and is a nice segue to a good dessert.

4 SERVINGS

3/4 cup (1 recipe) creamy yogurt dressing (pg 185)
2 heads curly, red lettuce, washed and dried
1 cup red seedless grapes, halved
2 ounces shaved parmesan (see tips, pgs 38–39)

1. Prepare the dressing in a large bowl.

2. When ready to serve, toss the dry lettuce leaves with the dressing and arrange on a platter or individual serving plates.

3. Top with the grapes and cheese shavings, and serve.

pasta salad with chevre,
mushrooms, and tomatoes

White balsamic vinaigrette, oregano, and chevre are a fantastic combination, and the seasoned mushrooms are a perfect match with the tomatoes and pasta. You can also use the mushroom-cheese-tomato mixture to fill a tart or pie shell, a phyllo basket, or a lettuce wrap for hors d'oeuvres. I have also served the mushroom-tomato-vinaigrette mixture with the chevre on the side to spread over sliced baguettes.

2 SERVINGS

1/4 cup (1 recipe) white balsamic vinaigrette (pg 186)
5 cups water
1 3/4 teaspoons salt
1 1/2 teaspoons cooking oil
1 1/2 cups rotini, radiatori, or any short pasta
1/2 pound mushrooms
1 tablespoon olive oil
1 teaspoon oregano leaves
1/8 teaspoon freshly ground black pepper
2 medium tomatoes, seeded and diced
3 ounces fresh chevre cheese, crumbled

1. Prepare the vinaigrette in a large bowl and set aside.

2. Bring the water to a boil in a saucepan over high heat. Add 1 1/2 teaspoons of the salt, cooking oil, and pasta. Cook until al dente. Drain the pasta, add to the vinaigrette, and allow to cool.

3. Preheat the broiler. Clean the mushrooms, cut into quarters, and place on a broiler pan. Drizzle with the olive oil, oregano, pepper, and the remaining salt. Broil for 7 to 8 minutes. Set aside to cool.

4. Mix the tomatoes with the cooled mushrooms.

5. When ready to serve, add the mushroom-tomato mixture and cheese to the pasta, toss gently and serve.

roasted vegetables
with white balsamic dressing

These beautifully colored, roasted veggies are tasty and crunchy. Refrigerate in a jar or nonreactive container for up to ten days and use for mozzarella sandwiches, pasta salads, stir-fries, and side dishes.

2 SERVINGS

1/4 cup (1 recipe) white balsamic vinaigrette (pg 186)
1 roasted red, orange, or yellow bell pepper
1/2 pound whole mushrooms
1 large onion
1 garlic clove
1 sprig thyme
2 1/2 tablespoons olive oil
1/4 teaspoon salt
1/8 teaspoon freshly ground black pepper
4 slices toasted Italian bread, optional

1. In a large bowl, prepare the vinaigrette (using thyme instead of cilantro), but do not add the oil, and set aside. Preheat the broiler.

2. Cut the pepper into 1/4-inch slices, clean the mushrooms, cut the onion into eighths, and slice the garlic. Place the vegetables in a bowl with the thyme sprig, add the olive oil, and toss gently.

3. Add the salt and pepper and toss again to mix well. Transfer to a broiler pan and broil for 10 minutes.

4. Add the warm roasted vegetables to the vinaigrette and toss to coat.

5. Serve with toasted bread slices or alone as a side dish.

TIP: When doubling the recipe, the cooking time is the same.

pecan, blue cheese, and pear salad

Pecans and coffee are a great flavor combination. Carry some pecans with you for a snack—they're an instant energy booster.

1/3 cup (1 recipe) creamy low-sugar red wine vinaigrette (pg 185)
1 small pear
3 cups torn curly, red lettuce, washed and dried
1/4 cup chopped caramelized coffee pecans (pg 28)
2 ounces blue cheese, crumbled

1. Prepare the vinaigrette in a medium bowl. Core and slice the pear. Place the slices into the vinaigrette until ready to serve.

2. Arrange the lettuce on a serving platter or individual plates. Top with the pear slices, sprinkle with the pecans and blue cheese, drizzle with the vinaigrette, and serve.

VARIATIONS: Cut the pear in half, scoop out the core, and fill with the blue cheese and pecans. Serve on the lettuce leaves, drizzled with the vinaigrette. Or, serve the pecans with the vinaigrette over chevre, sliced pears, or over sliced toast.

salmon and mandarin orange salad

Salmon and mandarin oranges are a wonderful match. I use their fresh, delicious, and natural great tastes in many recipes. Ginger is a must with these two.

4 SERVINGS

2/3 cup (1 recipe) asian vinaigrette (pg 184)
1 tablespoon pickled ginger, drained and julienned
2/3 cup mandarin orange or tangerine slices
8 ounces smoked salmon, thinly sliced
8 cups baby greens with arugula

1. Prepare the vinaigrette and add the ginger.

2. Place orange or tangerine slices and salmon on a platter and add the dressing. Let stand for 10 minutes or more.

3. When ready to serve, toss the greens with the salmon, orange or tangerine slices, and vinaigrette. Arrange on a serving platter or individual plates.

sherry, white raisin,
and pine nut salad

This green side salad is simple yet very flavorful. Take it with you for lunch or a snack. The nuts and raisins will give you energy. Try it topped with parmesan cheese shavings.

1/3 cup (1 recipe) sherry vinaigrette (pg 186)
2 tablespoons white raisins, chopped
1 tablespoon amaretto
3 cups torn Boston or Bibb lettuce, washed and dried
1/4 cup pine nuts, toasted*
2 tablespoons basil, julienned (about 20 leaves)*

1. Prepare the vinaigrette in a medium bowl. Cook the raisins and amaretto in a small pan until the amaretto has been absorbed. Add to the vinaigrette and set aside.

2. Arrange the lettuce on a serving platter or individual plates. Sprinkle with the pine nuts and basil, pour on the dressing, and serve.

*See tips, pgs 38–39

spiced almond
and brie salad

A very elegant salad— use mesclun or curly, red lettuce and serve it in miniature bowls for a cocktail party (this recipe yields about 8 small bowls). Serve the dressing with each bowl or on the side.

2 SERVINGS

1/3 cup (1 recipe) creamy low-sugar red wine vinaigrette (pg 185)
2 to 3 cups chopped romaine lettuce, washed and dried
1/3 cup (1/2 recipe) spiced caramelized almonds (pg 28)
2 ounces brie cheese, diced

1. Prepare the vinaigrette in a large bowl.

2. Toss the lettuce in the vinaigrette and arrange on a serving platter or individual plates.

3. Sprinkle with the almonds and cheese, and serve.

TIP: Freeze the cheese for 10 to 15 minutes to make cutting easier.

smoked tuna

and enoki salad

Enoki mushrooms are beautiful, crunchy, and very simple to use. They go well with many foods— try cooking with them and impress your friends and family!

2 SERVINGS

1/4 cup (1 recipe) white balsamic vinaigrette (pg 186)
1 3 1/2-ounce package enoki mushrooms
4 ounces smoked tuna, thinly sliced
4 cups torn mixed greens, washed and dried
1/2 cup watercress (leaves only)
2 tablespoons savory coffee syrup (pg 37)

1. Prepare the vinaigrette in a medium bowl. Rinse and trim the ends of the mushrooms. Mix the greens and watercress in a medium bowl.

2. Place the mushrooms and tuna in the vinaigrette for 10 minutes.

3. When ready to serve, strain the vinaigrette over the greens and watercress and toss to coat. Arrange the greens and watercress on a serving platter or individual plates.

4. Top with the tuna and mushrooms, and serve drizzled with the savory coffee syrup.

*onion
quiche with*
balsamic
reduction
sauce

This is a great recipe to serve in the evening and then take to work for lunch the next day. You can also freeze one of the quiches.

1 recipe basic coffee pie dough (pg 25)
2 eggs, beaten (whole or separated)

CARAMELIZED ONIONS
2 very large onions, thinly sliced (about 2 pounds)
2 tablespoons olive oil
1 tablespoon butter
1/2 teaspoon salt
1/4 teaspoon pepper
1/3 cup (doubled recipe) balsamic reduction sauce (pg 32) (divided use)

FILLING
1 cup whole milk
1 cup heavy cream
3 eggs
1 teaspoon salt
1/4 teaspoon pepper
Pinch nutmeg

1 1/2 cups shredded Swiss cheese
Cilantro sprigs, for decoration

2 9-inch tart pans

1. Prepare the dough and allow to rest in the refrigerator for 30 to 45 minutes. Preheat the oven to 375°F.

2. Cut the dough in half, roll to 1/8-inch thickness, set one over each tart pan, and cut off the over-hanging dough. Place foil over the dough, fill with beans or weights, and bake 15 to 20 minutes, or until golden. (You may keep the beans for future crusts.) Remove the foil, brush the shells with the beaten eggs, and set aside to cool to room temperature. Turn the oven to 425°.

3. To carmelize the onions, place them in a large sauté pan over medium heat with the olive oil and butter. Add the salt and pepper, cover, and cook for 10 minutes, or until translucent. Remove the lid and continue to cook until golden, about 10 minutes. Add 4 tablespoons of the balsamic reduction sauce and cook for 3 minutes. Set aside to cool for 5 to 10 minutes.

4. To prepare the filling, mix the milk, cream, eggs, salt, pepper, and nutmeg in a medium bowl with a fork or whisk and set aside.

5. In each pastry shell, place half of the onions, sprinkle with half of the cheese, add half of the filling, and decorate with cilantro sprigs.

6. Bake at 425°F for 25 to 30 minutes, or until set and lightly golden. Serve drizzled with the remaining balsamic reduction sauce.

203

greens
and
more

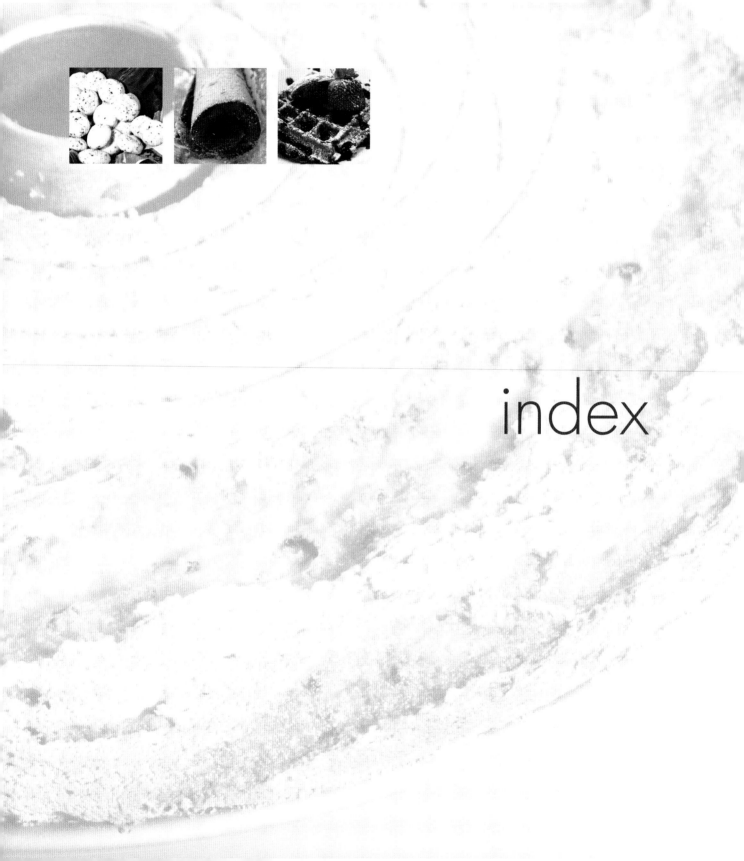

index

passion
for
coffee

211

entree

frostings, fillings, & icings

fruits

ice cream

lamb

milk & *dulce de leche*

classic *café con leche* or *café latté*, 148

coffee milk shakes
  dulce de leche, 152
  mocha, 152

dulce de leche, 24

dulce de leche and coffee natilla, 145

dulce de leche and coffee squares, 70

dulce de leche cake, 105

four milks coffee delight, 108

hot milk cake, 94

spiced *café con leche*
  cinnamon-allspice, 155
  cinnamon-cloves, 155
  vanilla-nutmeg, 155

three milks coffee delight, 106

mousse

bombe with white chocolate–coffee mousse, 138

caramel coffee mousse, 134

mamina's coffee mousse with mocha-rum sauce, 133

mocha mousse cups, 136

passion fruit and coffee mousse, 135

white chocolate and coffee berry mousse cups, 139

white chocolate–coffee mousse and shots, 137

nuts

all-whites macadamia coffee cake, 90

caramel coffee sauce with macadamia or amaretto, 33

caramel macadamia sauce, 33

chicken with dried apricots and pine nuts, 173

coffee macadamia ice cream (cooked), 122

coffee praline ice cream (uncooked), 121

ice cream-coffee sundae party, 125

sherry, white raisin, and pine nut salad, 200

passion fruit

all-whites mocha waffles with passion fruit sauce, 45

jumbo shrimp with savory passion fruit sauce, 180

passion fruit and coffee mousse, 135

passion fruit sauce I and II, 34

pecan

caramel pecan cake, 98

caramelized coffee pecans, 28

oooh! pecan phyllo bites, 74

pecan, blue cheese, and pear salad, 198

pecan coffee tart, 86

squid salad with caramelized coffee pecans, 194

pork

mango and prosciutto salad, 193

pork chops with sesame sauce, 169

pork tenderloins with dijon mustard sauce, 167

pork tenderloins with port wine sauce, 168

poultry

chicken with dried apricots and pine nuts, 173

coffee curried chicken, 172

cornish game hens with blackberry-coffee sauce, 170

sylvia's honey-mustard chicken strips, 174

tamarind-spiced chicken breasts, 175

syrup

vegetables

yellow gooseberry

Patricia McCausland-Gallo is a nutritionist, pastry chef, teacher, and food writer born in the Caribbean town of Barranquilla, Colombia. She has a B.S. in Foods and Nutrition from Louisiana State University, attended a School for Retort Operations, and completed courses of instruction prescribed by the Food and Drug Administration. She has attended the American Institute of Baking in Kansas as well as the École Lenôtre in Paris. Pachi, as she is called, has been a food writer for local and national newspapers in Colombia and now works and lives in Panama City, where she writes for *La Prensa*, a newspaper in the capital city, and for *Bajareque Times*, a newspaper in the coffee zone of Boquete, Panama. She has published two cookbooks: *Secrets of Colombian Cooking* (Hippocrene Books, 2004) and *Pasión por el Café* (Editorial Norma, 2006). She has been an executive pastry chef, a manager, and an owner of bakeries in Barranquilla and Cali. She also develops recipes for healthy teens and special needs children.

Other titles by Patricia McCausland Gallo:

Pasion por el café (Spanish)
ISBN 958-04-9252-2

Secrets of Colombian Cooking
ISBN 0-7818-1025-6

Secretos de la cocina colombiana (Spanish)
ISBN 978-958-44-0232-5

Juangui Goes to College
ISBN 978-0-9797594-1-3

Available at www.amazon.com or www.creativeculinary.net.